THE LAST ELIJAH MESSAGE

THE LAST ELIJAH MESSAGE:

Essentials for Revival

Doug Batchelor

Published by:
Amazing Facts, Inc.
PO Box 1058
Roseville, CA 95678-8058

Edited by Anthony Lester
Original editing by Debra Hicks for *The Last Elijah Message, The Last Tower of Babel, The Facets of Faith, Fig Leaves and Pharisees, The Peril of Smooth Things, A Real Sacrifice, Reviving Dry Bones, The Secret Weapon, What Shall I Wear?*; and Alicia Goree for *A Perfect Christian?, Power in Purity*

Cover Design by Haley Trimmer
Layout by Greg Solie - Altamont Graphics
Final Copy Proofing by Tarah Solie

ISBN # 1-58019-155-X

Table of Contents

Preface

As the Lord Jesus Christ ascended into heaven, He left the church with the charge to *"Go ye therefore, and teach all nations, baptizing them in the name of the Father, and of the Son, and of the Holy Ghost"* (Matthew 28:19). This is the first priority and most essential duty of every Christian. Of course, He did not leave us empty handed, without tools, in this Great Commission. *"I tell you the truth; It is expedient for you that I go away: for if I go not away, the Comforter will not come unto you; but if I depart, I will send him unto you. And when he is come, he will reprove the world of sin, and of righteousness, and of judgment"* (John 16:7). As Christians, we can act with complete confidence that with the Holy Spirit, we have been given the power to help rescue a world lost and trapped in the grip of darkness.

Yet as the Lord tarries, allowing time for all to hear His message, many churches and individuals are struggling to remain on fire for this task. It is strange, to say in the least, that the gift of everlasting life can lose its force of conviction in everyday life. Yet sadly, this is the story of the human race—to see this, we need only to read the story of the disciples sleeping while Jesus prayed in the garden, even after showing them miracle after miracle of His power. We can also look to God's first church, the Jewish nation, who lost faith while Moses tarried on the mountain, even after God sent the plagues, parted the Red Sea, and revealed His glory in the pillar of fire to rescue them from Egypt.

If you are someone who, like the virgins in the parable of the tarrying bridegroom (Matthew 25), has somehow let your light go out in the midst of a busy life of family, finances and work, do not be dismayed. You are not alone. As much as it has been an ailment for humans throughout history, God has always had the perfect medicine. He wants to relight your fire.

Prior to Jesus, when the Jewish nation yearned for a Messiah, they became impatient of searching through Scriptures for what that Son of Man would offer. Instead, spiritually asleep, they dreamed of their own kind of rescue from the Romans, and this worldly view distracted them from their spiritual commission. They became drowsy and somehow missed the Savior for which they had waited so long.

Yet, like every other time the Jews lost sight of the Prize, God provided a messenger to get them back on track. He sent faithful followers like Elijah, Elisha and John the Baptist. These prophets, under the guiding influence of the spirit, revived the Jewish people, breathing life into a once dead body. They were sent to *"prepare the way for the LORD."*

And now the Father in heaven wants to do that for you today. His church has fallen asleep, pursuing its own lazy dream of His return, even in the midst of prophecy being rapidly fulfilled. So this collection of articles is designed to stir the church—and you personally—from the drowsiness of waiting on the Lord, into reactivated participants in spreading the gospel. If you've lost sight of the Prize, if your light has been dimmed and your fire cooled, God is calling you to be a part of today's Elijah Message, and bring revival into your heart and the spirit of your church.

This collection is dedicated to those great prophets of revival and follows in the tradition of setting the hearts of God's people on fire for His glory, forever and ever.

THE LAST ELIJAH MESSAGE
CHAPTER ONE

An Amazing Fact: Scientists tell us that the sound waves set in motion by our voices go on an endless journey through space, and that, if we had the power to stand on some planet long years afterward with instruments delicate enough, we might be able to find them again and recreate the words we spoke here on earth.

People need heroes—great men and women we can look up to as role models and mentors.

Ministries need heroes too. The kings and prophets from long ago who proclaimed special messages and exuded faithful courage provide excellent heroes whom we can emulate. And *Amazing Facts* has chosen two of the greatest prophets in the Holy Writ as our designated heroes—Elijah and John the Baptist.

The last words of the Old Testament make known a stirring and powerful prophecy that has often been misunderstood. Take a moment to become familiar with this passage for with the Spirit's help, we intend to bring new life to these words:

"Behold, I will send you Elijah the prophet before the coming of the great and dreadful day of the LORD: And he shall turn the heart of the fathers to the children, and the heart of the children to their fathers, lest I come and smite the earth with a curse" (Malachi 4:5, 6).

REINCARNATION?

Perhaps we should first spend a moment understanding what this verse does not mean. In the time of Jesus, many believed that Elijah would literally come back down from heaven to live again on earth, or possibly be reborn into a new man. Jesus once asked the disciples, *"Whom say the people that I am? They answering said, John the Baptist; but some say, Elias* [the Greek form of Elijah]*; and others say, that one of the old prophets is risen again"* (Luke 9:18, 19).

The Jews lived with a sense of expectancy that Elijah would soon come to announce the advent of the Messiah. But this prophecy in Malachi was never intended to imply that the Old Testament prophet would return to the earth.

Instead, it was Elijah's spirit of revival and reform that was predicted to return. Speaking of the birth of John the Baptist, the angel Gabriel said to Zacharias, *"And he shall go before him in the spirit and power of Elias, to turn the hearts of the fathers to the children, and the disobedient to the wisdom of the just; to make ready a people prepared for the Lord"* (Luke 1:17).

Gabriel was the first to point out that John the Baptist fulfilled the prophecy in Malachi. John was to precede the Lord to do a special work of revival and reform. Jesus later confirmed this fact when He said, *"For all the prophets and the law prophesied until John. And if ye will receive it, this is Elias, which was for to come"* (Matthew 11:13, 14).

However, the completion of Malachi's prophecy does not end with John the Baptist. There is also a modern-day fulfillment. Notice the prophecy says: *"I will send you Elijah the prophet before the coming of the great and dreadful day of the LORD."* The *"great and dreadful day of the LORD,"* which is also called *"the great day of His wrath"* in Revelation 6:17, is synonymous with the second coming. So this other fulfillment points us to a period just prior to the return of Jesus!

SPIRIT AND POWER OF ELIJAH

To better understand this prophecy, we need to go back to the time of Elijah. Here we discover that the first person filled with the *"spirit and power of Elijah"* was not John the Baptist, but rather Elisha, the servant of Elijah.

When God revealed that He was taking Elijah up to heaven soon, Elisha asked that he might receive a double portion of Elijah's spirit. *"Elisha said, I pray thee, let a double portion of thy spirit be upon me. And he [Elijah] said, Thou hast asked a hard thing: nevertheless, if thou see me when I am taken from thee, it shall be so unto thee; but if not, it shall not be so"* (2 Kings 2:9, 10).

As Elisha witnessed Elijah's rapture, he was baptized with the double portion of Elijah's spirit that he requested. *"And when the sons of the prophets which were to view at Jericho saw him, they said, The spirit of Elijah doth rest on Elisha"* (2 Kings 2:15).

What will the Spirit and power of Elijah do? *"He shall turn the heart of the fathers to the children, and the heart of the children to their fathers"* (Malachi 4:6).

In a literal sense, real revival brings a new expression of love to the family and then spreads from there into the community. The most basic unit of any society, government, or church is the family. The outpouring of God's Spirit will always result in love that leads to obedience of His commandments. Jesus said, *"If ye love me, keep my commandments"* (John 14:15).

Of course, this includes the commands that say: *"Honor thy father and thy mother"* and *"Fathers, provoke not your children to anger, lest they be discouraged"* (Exodus 20:12; Colossians 3:21).

The Elijah message will bring the power of love and blessing into the families who receive it, and a curse on those who reject it (Malachi 4:6). *"I the LORD thy God am a jealous God, visiting the iniquity of the fathers upon the children unto the third and fourth generation of them that hate me; And shewing mercy unto thousands of them that love me, and keep my commandments"* (Exodus 20:5, 6).

Notice that the angel Gabriel rewords the prophecy in Luke 1:16, 17: *"And many of the children of Israel shall he turn to the Lord their God. And he shall go before him in the spirit and power of Elias, to turn the hearts of the fathers to the children, and the disobedient to the wisdom of the just; to make ready a people prepared for the Lord."*

So in a spiritual sense, the Elijah message will also work to unite disobedient earthly children with their heavenly Father.

12 CHARACTERISTICS OF THE ELIJAH MESSAGE

Let's look at the 12 outstanding characteristics of Elijah and John the Baptist that will also be present in the last days. Amazing Facts has adopted these points as a prominent part of its mission.

1. They were bold and fearless in preaching, even before kings.
Elijah—Elijah told Ahab, *"I have not troubled Israel; but thou, and thy father's house, in that ye have forsaken the commandments of the LORD, and thou hast followed Baalim"* (1 Kings 18:18).
John—*"John had said unto Herod, It is not lawful for thee to have thy brother's wife"* (Mark 6:18).

Both John the Baptist and Elijah were fearless in preaching a straight message before rulers and governments. Jesus said this would happen again in the last days. *"Ye shall be brought before rulers and kings for my sake, for a testimony against them"* (Mark 13:9).

We must not seek to find our approval among men, but rather with God. To establish a great revival, the Elijah message must be a bold proclamation of clear, uncompromising, and sometimes unpopular truth.

"For the time will come when they will not endure sound doctrine; but after their own lusts shall they heap to themselves teachers, having itching ears; And they shall turn away their ears from the truth, and shall be turned unto fables" (2 Timothy 4:3, 4).

2. They had a simple diet and lifestyle.

Elijah—*"Bring me, I pray thee, a morsel of bread in thine hand"* (1 Kings 17:11).

John—*"He did eat locusts and wild honey"* (Mark 1:6).

Both Elijah and John were known for their simple diets and wilderness living. These basic rigors kept their mental faculties clear and their bodies strong, that they might be prepared for the special work God called them to do.

Likewise, the church in the last days must be revived to the truth that there is a strong connection between the body and the spirit. What we eat and drink, as well as our personal living habits, has a direct effect on our mental clarity and ability to discern truth. The power to resist temptation can be traced in part to a simple diet and moderate lifestyle. Remember, sin came on the human race as a result of eating the wrong thing.

"Blessed art thou, O land, when thy king is the son of nobles, and thy princes eat in due season, for strength, and not for drunkenness!" (Ecclesiastes 10:17).

"Whether therefore ye eat, or drink, or whatsoever ye do, do all to the glory of God" (1 Corinthians 10:31).

3. They dressed in modest, simple clothing.

Elijah—*"He was an hairy man* [with a garment of hair], *and girt with a girdle* [belt] *of leather about his loins* [waist]*"* (2 Kings 1:8).

John—*"And John was clothed with camel's hair, and with a girdle of a skin* [leather belt] *about his loins* [waist]" (Mark 1:6).

In a time when kings and priests loved to wear ornaments and long, flowing robes, Elijah and John's modesty and simplicity were a stinging rebuke.

We live in an age where there has never been more arrogant attention given to flamboyance and fashion. The main goal of modern clothing designers is to highlight a person's sexuality. Sadly, everything from body piercing to tattoos is being indulged even among professed Christians. Once again, the church desperately needs last-day Elijahs to witness for Christ by their example of humility and simplicity through modest clothing and appearance.

"Put on the new man, which after God is created in righteousness and true holiness" (Ephesians 4:24). *"In like manner also, that women adorn themselves in modest apparel, with shamefacedness* [propriety] *and sobriety* [moderation]; *not with broided hair, or gold, or pearls, or costly array* [clothing]" (1 Timothy 2:9).

4. They believed in discipling others.

Elijah—*"So he departed thence, and found Elisha… and Elijah passed by him, and cast his mantle upon him"* (1 Kings 19:19).

John—*"And the disciples of John shewed him of all these things"* (Luke 7:18).

The Scriptures record that Elijah not only discipled Elisha, but he also visited the schools of the prophets (also translated *"the disciples of the prophets"*), which were scattered all through the land of Israel (2 Kings 2). These training centers combined spiritual instruction with practical work skills, and the young men trained there went throughout Israel to teach others the ways of God.

John, likewise, reproduced his faith by teaching the disciples who followed him. Both John and Elijah spent most of their time training not the priests and Levites, but rather the common people. Similarly, the last great movement of God will not be led by clergy alone, but also by Spirit-filled laypersons. This is why the Elijah message must give attention to training, discipling and mobilizing every member of God's church.

5. They preached a baptism of repentance and death to self.

Elijah—*"And Elijah said unto him, Tarry, I pray thee, here; for the* LORD *hath sent me to Jordan"* (2 Kings 2:6).

John—*"Then went out to him Jerusalem, and all Judea, and all the region round about Jordan, And were baptized of him in Jordan, confessing their sins"* (Matthew 3:5, 6).

One identifying mark of the Elijah message is that it calls people to the Jordan River—a symbol of repentance and baptism. The children of Israel had to cross the Jordan to enter the Promised Land, just as we enter the waters of baptism and cross over to a new life. The great commission of Jesus to the church will have its finest hour in the future, when once again modern Elijahs will baptize converts to Christ in explosive, Pentecostal-like numbers.

"Then went he down, and dipped himself seven times in Jordan, according to the saying of the man of God: and his flesh came again like unto the flesh of a little child, and he was clean" (2 Kings 5:14).

"Go ye therefore, and teach all nations, baptizing them in the name of the Father, and of the Son, and of the Holy Ghost" (Matthew 28:19).

6. They both manifested humility.

Elijah—*"And Elijah went up to the top of Carmel; and he cast himself down upon the earth, and put his face between his knees"* (1 Kings 18:42).

John—*"He that cometh after me is mightier than I, whose shoes I am not worthy to bear"* (Matthew 3:11).

Before Jesus comes again, the people of God will have learned to reflect the meek and humble character of Jesus in an age of arrogance and pride.

"He hath shewed thee, O man, what is good; and what doth the LORD *require of thee, but to do justly, and to love mercy, and to walk humbly with thy God?"* (Micah 6:8).

7. They both endured religious persecution.

Elijah—*"Then Jezebel sent a messenger to Elijah, saying, So let the gods do to me, and more also, if I make not thy life as the life of one of them [who had been killed] by to morrow about this time"* (1 Kings 19:2).

John—*"And she went forth, and said unto her mother [Herodias], What shall I ask? And she said, The head of John the Baptist"* (Mark 6:24).

In the Old Testament, a pagan queen named Jezebel married Ahab, the king of Israel. Jezebel and her daughter, Athaliah, persecuted God's people and tried to entice Ahab to kill Elijah and the other prophets.

In the New Testament, Herodias, the pagan wife of king Herod, and her daughter Salome succeeded in enticing Herod to kill John the Baptist.

The persecution experienced by Elijah and John will soon be repeated. In the last days, Revelation tells us the *"Mother of harlots"* and her daughters will persecute God's remnant people, the last-day Elijahs.

"And the dragon was wroth with the woman, and went to make war with the remnant of her seed, which keep the commandments of God, and have the testimony of Jesus Christ" (Revelation 12:17).

"And upon her forehead was a name written, MYSTERY, BABYLON THE GREAT, THE MOTHER OF HARLOTS AND ABOMINATIONS OF THE EARTH. And I saw the woman drunken with the blood of the saints, and with the blood of the martyrs of Jesus" (Revelation 17:5, 6).

8. They both ran before the king.

Elijah—*"And the hand of the* LORD *was on Elijah; and he girded up his loins, and ran before Ahab to the entrance of Jezreel"* (1 Kings 18:46).

John—*"As it is written in the book of the words of Esaias [Isaiah] the prophet, saying, The voice of one crying in the wilderness, Prepare ye the way of the Lord, make his paths straight"* (Luke 3:4).

When a monarch traveled in Bible times, servants often ran ahead to prepare the path for the approaching king. They cleared the road of rocks and obstacles, filled in potholes, cut down high spots, and straightened the crooked turns.

In the same way, those preaching the Elijah message in the last days will help prepare people for the coming of our King Jesus. They will proclaim a message that makes the way of salvation clear, plain, and easy to understand.

"And I saw another angel fly in the midst of heaven, having the everlasting gospel to preach unto them that dwell on the earth, and to every nation, and kindred, and tongue, and people" (Revelation 14:6).

9. They were both supremely interested in glorifying God.

Elijah—*"Hear me, O LORD, hear me, that this people may know that thou art the LORD God, and that thou hast turned their heart back again"* (1 Kings 18:37).

John—*"He must increase, but I must decrease"* (John 3:30).

Those preaching the Elijah message will make glorifying God their top priority. They will be wholly consecrated to God's cause, just as were John and Elijah. They will be willing to make any sacrifice that others might be saved—in other words, to spend and be spent in the work of God.

"I beseech you therefore, brethren, by the mercies of God, that ye present your bodies a living sacrifice, holy, acceptable unto God, which is your reasonable service" (Romans 12:1).

10. They repaired the altar of God.

Elijah—*"And Elijah said unto all the people, Come near unto me. And all the people came near unto him. And he repaired the altar of the LORD that was broken down"* (1 Kings 18:30).

John—*"In those days came John the Baptist, preaching in the wilderness of Judaea, And saying, Repent ye: for the kingdom of heaven is at hand"* (Matthew 3:1, 2).

The Elijah message will be a trumpet call to return to *"the faith which was once delivered unto the saints"* (Jude 1:3). Today, when so many are telling us that the teachings of the Bible are old-fashioned and need to be revised to better fit the times, we desperately need to be reminded that God said, *"For I am the LORD, I change not"* (Malachi 3:6).

"And they that shall be of thee shall build the old waste places: thou shalt raise up the foundations of many generations; and thou shalt be called, The repairer of the breach, The restorer of paths to dwell in" (Isaiah 58:12).

11. Their messages sparked revival and reformation.

Elijah—*"Now therefore send, and gather to me all Israel unto mount Carmel. … And Elijah came unto all the people, and said, How long halt ye between two opinions? if the LORD be God, follow him"* (1 Kings 18:19–21).

John—*"John did baptize in the wilderness, and preach the baptism of repentance for the remission of sins. And there went out unto him all the land of Judaea, and they of Jerusalem, and were all baptized of him in the river of Jordan, confessing their sins"* (Mark 1:4, 5).

In the days of Elijah and John the Baptist, God's people had been corrupted by the pagan influences around them and had compromised God's truth (1 Kings 19:14; Matthew 3:1, 2). These two brave prophets delivered a message that sparked revival and reform among God's people.

Today, once again, it seems that much of Christianity is lukewarm and worldly. If judgment is going to begin at God's house (Ezekiel 9:6; 1 Peter 4:17), then certainly the revival must start there too! Since God's plan is for His people to reach the entire world, He must first send the Elijah message to reach the church.

In the Old Testament, Elijah led the people to repent and turn back to God on mount Carmel. Then he prayed, and God sent abundant rain to end the drought. Likewise, John the Baptist called on the people of his day to repent and accept Jesus. Then shortly thereafter, they received the former rain of the Holy Spirit on Pentecost. Modern Elijahs will also preach a message of repentance. Then, when the church humbles itself, the latter rain of God's Spirit will fall.

12. **The Elijah message will point people to Christ.**
   Elijah—*"Elijah the prophet came near, and said, LORD God of Abraham, Isaac, and of Israel, let it be known this day that thou art God"* (1 Kings 18:36).
   John—*"The next day John seeth Jesus coming unto him, and saith, Behold the Lamb of God, which taketh away the sin of the world"* (John 1:29).

The burning desire of modern Elijahs will be to turn people to Jesus, that they might know Him and have everlasting life.

GOD'S ARMY

If the Lord felt it was important to send a special messenger to prepare Israel for Jesus' first coming, how much more important is it for Him to send a special message and messengers to awaken the church for Jesus' second coming—the very climax of redemption?

In the same way that the Lord empowered Elijah, Elisha and John the Baptist to do a work of revival and preparation, God is today preparing an army of last-day Elijahs to do a great work of revival! *Amazing Facts* invites you to be a part of delivering this great, end-time Elijah message-*"to make ready a people prepared for the Lord"* (Luke 1:17).

CRUCIFIED WITH CHRIST
CHAPTER TWO

An Amazing Fact: As an unusual way to draw attention to world peace, in 1973 Patrice Tamao of the Dominican Republic allowed himself to be crucified as thousands watched. On television, Tamao had three six-inch stainless steel nails driven through his hands and feet—he intended to stay on the cross for 48 hours. However, after 20 hours he requested to be taken down because he had developed an infection.

Jesus told His disciples, *"If any man will come after me, let him deny himself, and take up his cross daily, and follow me"* (Luke 9:23). Later, the apostle Paul repeated this theme. *"I am crucified with Christ: nevertheless I live; yet not I, but Christ liveth in me: and the life which I now live in the flesh I live by the faith of the Son of God, who loved me, and gave himself for me"* (Galatians 2:20).

From the time of Christ's sacrifice to the present, many have sought to show their devotion to Jesus, secure their own forgiveness, or make some public statement by actually having themselves crucified. In 1965, Daniel Waswa in Kenya compelled his wife to crucify him "for the sins of all Kenyans." After reluctantly obeying, his wife collapsed and died—apparently from shock. Daniel was rescued by neighbors, but he later died from an infection. Does the Lord require this kind of literal fanaticism when He calls us to take up our cross and follow Him?

To better understand these profound passages regarding the cross, we need to turn to the only story in the Bible where we find a chilling telling of this dreaded method of execution. As we examine the Gospel accounts of the crucifixion, we quickly notice that Jesus did not die alone. Two other men were "crucified with Christ" that day.

Countless lessons can be drawn from the experience of the thieves who died flanking the Savior—and especially the one who accepted Jesus. All four Gospel accounts tell of the two thieves who were crucified with Christ, but only Luke tells the story of the penitent thief who turned to Jesus in the final hours of his life. Let's begin by revisiting this popular passage: *"There were also two others, criminals, led with Him to be put to death. And when they had come to the place called Calvary, there they crucified Him, and the criminals, one on the right hand and the other on the left. ... Then one of the criminals who were hanged blasphemed Him, saying, 'If You are the Christ, save Yourself and us.' But the other, answering, rebuked him, saying, 'Do you not even fear God, seeing you are under the same condemnation? And we indeed justly, for we receive the due reward of our deeds; but this Man has done nothing wrong.' Then he said to Jesus, 'Lord, remember me when You come into Your kingdom.' And Jesus said to him, 'Assuredly, I say to you, today you will be with Me in Paradise' "* (Luke 23:32, 33, 39–43, NKJV).

ONLY TWO CHOICES

These two thieves represent the two great classes of people who have ever lived or ever will live—the saved and the lost, the righteous and the wicked. In His famous parable, Jesus compared them to sheep and goats (Matthew 25:31–46). The Son of Man set the sheep (the righteous) on His right hand, and the goats (the wicked) on His left. Since, in the Bible, the right hand represents favor (Matthew 26:64; Acts 2:32, 33), I believe that the thief who was saved was to the right of Jesus.

Notice the ways these two doomed men represent all people:
1. **They were both guilty of rebellion, murder, and stealing.** We too have *"sinned, and come short of the glory of God"* (Romans 3:23). We have rebelled against our Maker's will, committed murder in our hearts, and robbed God of the time, means, and talents He has lent to us.
2. **They could do nothing to save themselves.** Picture them hanging there naked, with their hands and feet spiked mercilessly to a cross. I cannot think of two individuals who were ever more utterly powerless to rescue themselves. We are just as helpless to save ourselves by our good works as were those two thieves to escape from the cross.
3. **They both had an equal opportunity to be saved.** Although

helpless to save themselves, these two men were in the immediate presence of the greatest dynamo of love and power in the whole cosmos. But salvation is not obtained by osmosis. To be helped, they had to first reach out in faith and ask Him. We too are ever in the presence of the Savior, and He is only a prayer away (Psalm 139:7). But many souls will be needlessly lost, while hoping and desiring to be saved, because they do not perform the simple act of asking.

BELIEVING THE EVIDENCE

W e are all saved by faith, and true faith is based on evidence; otherwise, it is simply a blind, reckless presumption. On the day of the crucifixion, a mountain of evidence was given to show that Jesus was the Son of God.

After the three crosses were hoisted into position and the initial shock associated with crucifixion set in, the Bible tells that at first, both of the criminals joined the mob in mocking Him. *"Even the robbers who were crucified with Him reviled Him"* (Matthew 27:44, NKJV). But as the agonizing hours dragged by, the thief on His right began to reflect on his wasted life and now-hopeless future. As he humbled himself, the Holy Spirit began to penetrate the man's contrite heart and urged him to consider the noble way Jesus bore His suffering. There was a growing conviction in the thief's mind that perhaps this was more than an ordinary man who was hanging a few feet away. Consider the following points:

- This man had almost certainly heard of Jesus' many miracles. Nearly everyone living in Palestine during that time—from Herod on his throne to the lowly beggar on the street—had heard of the wonderful works of mercy wrought by this carpenter from Nazareth. Even the noted Jewish historian Flavius Josephus spoke of the incredible miracles Jesus performed.

- When Pontius Pilate brought Barabbas and Jesus before the people, the thief likely noticed the marked contrast between their angry leader and the gentle Savior. He probably heard Pilate ask, *"What shall I do then with Jesus which is called*

Christ?" (Matthew 27:22). But even more important was Pilate's confession, *"I find no fault in this man"* (Luke 23:4).

● He probably overheard many believers in the crowd speak of Christ's miracles and great deeds.

● The thief heard Jesus forgive His enemies. It was almost an involuntary reflex to fight, struggle and curse as the spikes were being driven through the hands and feet. But the repentant thief clearly heard Jesus say, *"Father, forgive them; for they know not what they do"* (Luke 23:34). Like a lamb before slaughter, the Messiah made no effort to resist (Isaiah 53:7).

● He saw the Roman soldiers casting lots for Christ's garments at the foot of the cross, in direct fulfillment of King David's messianic prophecy: *"They part my garments among them, and cast lots upon my vesture"* (Psalm 22:18).

● He witnessed a supernatural darkness descend over the land in the middle of a spring day (Matthew 27:45).

● He read the sign directly above the head of Jesus, which declared: *"This is the King of the Jews"* (Luke 23:38).

As the evidence of Jesus' divine nature continues to mount, the thief on His right hand feels the Holy Spirit press on him. There is only one logical verdict. The long-awaited Messiah, the King of Israel, is hanging on the cross beside him. He is the One who came to fulfill the famous prophecy: *"But he was wounded for our transgressions, he was bruised for our iniquities: the chastisement for our peace was upon him; and with his stripes we are healed. ... And he made his grave with the wicked. ... And he was numbered with the transgressors; and he bare the sin of many, and made intercession for the transgressors"* (Isaiah 53:5, 9, 12).

Somehow this thief understands that Jesus is suffering for *"the transgressors"* and knows that he is in that category. In the classic book *The Desire of Ages*, we read: "Little by little the chain of evidence is joined together. In Jesus, bruised, mocked and hanging upon the cross, he sees the Lamb of God, that taketh away the sin of the world. Hope is mingled with anguish in his voice as the helpless, dying soul casts himself upon a dying Saviour" (p. 750).

The criminal on the left joins the taunting mob and shouts, "*If thou be the Christ, save thyself and us*" (Luke 23:39). But the repentant thief, aware that he is dying and has nothing to fear, now speaks in Jesus' defense. Turning to his former partner, he asks, "*Dost not thou fear God, seeing thou art in the same condemnation? And we indeed justly; for we receive the due reward of our deeds: but this man hath done nothing amiss*" (Luke 23:40, 41).

I can almost see a temporary silence fall on the mocking crowd as they listen to this unusual exchange. Then the repentant thief's final words pass through his parched, quivering lips. He calls out in clear, triumphant tones: "*Lord, remember me when thou comest into thy kingdom*" (verse 42). His famous plea begins with "*Lord*" and ends with "*kingdom*." He does not ask for justice, but mercy.

THE DEADLY "IF"

Please don't miss the fact that both thieves wanted to be saved. However, the thief on the Lord's left did not have a saving faith. He said, "*If thou be the Christ.*"

"If" is a neutralizing word when praying to the Lord of the universe. When tempting Jesus in the wilderness, the devil revealed his identity when he said, "*If thou be the Son of God*" (Matthew 4:3). Without faith, it is impossible to please God (Hebrews 11:6), and the word "if" neutralizes a person's faith.

Like much of the world, the thief on the left wanted salvation from the penalty of sin, but not from sin itself. He lacked a saving faith. Jesus says, "*If ye believe not that I am he, ye shall die in your sins*" (John 8:24).

The story of the thief on the cross serves as a microcosm for the plan of salvation. In the space of a few short verses (Luke 23:40–43), we see the believing thief pass through all the basic steps to salvation and experience all the elements necessary for conversion.

1. He saw Jesus lifted up. Jesus promises, "*And I, if I be lifted up from the earth, will draw all men unto me*" (John 12:32).
2. He believed in Christ as the spotless Lamb of God—a perfect atoning sacrifice. "*This Man has done nothing wrong*"

(Luke 23:41, NKJV).

3. He repented of his sins and confessed his guilt. *"And we indeed justly; for we receive the due reward of our deeds"* (verse 41).
4. He testified publicly, despite the prevailing ridicule, that Jesus was his Lord and King. *"Lord, ... thy kingdom"* (verse 42).
5. He asked for forgiveness. *"Lord, remember me"* (verse 42).
6. He suffered with Jesus.
7. He died with Christ, and in Christ.

Hungry to Save

Even though Jesus was suffering the most intense agony imaginable, He never failed to hear a sincere cry for help. In answer to the desperate plea *"Lord, remember me,"* Jesus says: *"Can a woman forget her nursing child, And not have compassion on the son of her womb? Surely they may forget, Yet I will not forget you. See, I have inscribed you on the palms of My hands"* (Isaiah 49:15, 16, NKJV).

In essence, Jesus was saying, "How could I forget you when I am hanging here for you?" The devil could nail His loving hands to a tree, but he could not prevent the Savior from saving. This dying thief's earnest petition was the lone glimmer of light allowed to penetrate the darkness and suffering that enveloped Jesus. The Messiah answered with love, compassion and power. *"Verily I say unto thee, To day shalt thou be with me in paradise"* (Luke 23:43).

In Jesus' final moments alive on the cross, the Father gave His Son the gift of seeing this wretched criminal transformed into a soul redeemed for eternity. For Jesus, it was blessed assurance that His life and sacrifice would not be in vain.

Hanging on Faith

After Jesus said, *"You will be with Me in paradise,"* a wonderful peace flooded the troubled soul of this repentant thief. I believe there was a marked change in his countenance. A great calm came over him as the terrible weight from all the sins of his life lifted from his heart and transferred to the Lamb of God beside him.

A few moments later, Jesus called out: *"It is finished!"* *"Father, into thy hands I commend my spirit"* (John 19:30; Luke 23:46). *"And when the centurion, which stood over against him, saw that he so cried out, and gave up the ghost, he said, Truly this man was the Son of God"* (Mark 15:39). The spontaneous testimony of this Roman soldier served as confirmation that the thief on the cross was not the only one who grasped the truth of Christ's divinity.

The weight of evidence was compelling, yet God always allows some room for doubt. After Jesus died, the penitent thief was left to face the mocking crowd alone. Despite the fact that his body still hung by nails, this man's soul now hung by faith in his Redeemer's word. At times we too must trust our salvation to a silent Savior.

IN PARADISE TODAY?

We can't rightfully study this story of the thief on the cross without taking a few lines to explain a common misunderstanding. Many have read Christ's promise to the thief in Luke 23:43 and concluded that the saved thief went to be with Jesus in Paradise that day. However, we know that isn't true because Jesus did not go to Paradise that day. After the resurrection, when He appeared to Mary and she clung to His feet in worship, Jesus said, *"Do not hold on to me, because I have not yet ascended to the Father"* (John 20:17, NRSV).

Then why did Jesus say, "Today you will be with me in Paradise"? The answer is that He didn't! The original Greek has no punctuation, which means that the translators of the King James put the comma in the wrong place.

It should read, "Assuredly, I say to you today, you will be with Me in Paradise." The emphasis was on the word "today." In other words, He told the thief, "I am promising you today, even though I do not look like a victorious Lord and King, that there will be a place reserved for you in my kingdom."

DEAD TO SIN

As a prank, a friend sent me a gift certificate good for "one free visit to the infamous Dr. Jack Kevorkian," more commonly known as Dr. Death. Some people are so tired of hurting that they would rather commit suicide than continue living in pain.

In one sense, suicide is exactly what it means to be *"crucified with Christ."* However, the solution to the sin problem is not physical suicide, but ego suicide. Paul says, *"For he that is dead is freed from sin"* (Romans 6:7). Dead people do not get offended or lose their tempers. Dead people do not behave selfishly or harbor bitterness and grudges. Dietrich Bonhoeffer said, "When Christ calls a man, he bids him come and die."

God's Word declares: *"Those who are Christ's have crucified the flesh with its passions and desires"* (Galatians 5:24, NKJV). In Romans 6:11, we read, *"Likewise reckon ye also yourselves to be dead indeed unto sin, but alive unto God through Jesus Christ our Lord."*

A.W. Tozer said, "The man with a cross no longer controls his destiny; he lost control when he picked up his cross. That cross immediately became to him an all-absorbing interest, an overwhelming interference. No matter what he may desire to do, there is but one thing he can do; that is, move on toward the place of crucifixion."

THE SCARS OF SIN

Many years ago, Karla Fay Tucker became the first woman executed in Texas since the Civil War. While on death row for a gruesome murder, she experienced a complete conversion and became a model prisoner. She was even forgiven by her victim's family. Nevertheless, Karla Fay Tucker was still given her lethal injection on schedule.

We must not miss the fact that accepting Jesus does not always remove the consequences of our sins nor erase the ugly scars. The result of our sins often linger long after we have received forgiveness. On this point, the repentant thief on the cross is again a fitting example. Christ's forgiveness did not spare him from an agonizing death on the cross. The salvation he received that day was salvation from the ultimate penalty for sin, not from all its temporal consequences.

DEATHBED CONVERSIONS

Did you know that this is the only story in the Bible of a "deathbed conversion"? This one example is recorded so none need lose hope of salvation—even in the end; but there is only one example so none would recklessly presume it is safe to wait till the bitter end. I am convinced that one of two things happens to people who purposely plan on turning to Jesus in the last hours of their life. Either they never can, or they never will.

To say, "I will give my life and strength and means to the devil and then, in the last fleeting moments of my earthly existence, I will turn to God" is the highest insult a mortal can offer God. It is something like offering an ugly, thorny rose stem to your spouse after all the beautiful, fragrant petals have fallen off.

Repentance is a gift from God (Acts 5:31; 2 Timothy 2:24, 25). We cannot predict when we are going to repent. If we have spent our lives spurning the loving invitations of the Holy Spirit, it may be that when the end comes, we will find we have grieved away the Comforter and lost our capacity to repent. *"How shall we escape, if we neglect so great salvation?"* (Hebrews 2:3). Then, of course, there is the very real possibility that we could die suddenly with no warning, and thus be unable to repent.

STARTING AT THE CROSS

Officer Peter O'Hanlon was patrolling on night duty in northern England some years ago when he heard a quivering sob. Turning, he saw in the shadows a little boy sitting on a doorstep. With tears rolling down his cheeks, the child whimpered, "I'm lost. Please take me home."

"Where do you live, child? What street?" the officer asked.

"I don't know," the little boy moaned.

The policeman began naming street after street, trying to help him remember where he lived. When that failed, he repeated the names of the shops and hotels in the area, but all without success. Then he remembered that in the center of the city was a well-known church with a large white cross that towered high above the surrounding landscape. He pointed to it and asked, "Do you live anywhere near that?"

The boy's face immediately brightened. "Yes sir, take me to the cross. I can find my way home from there!" We will never find the way to our heavenly home unless we begin our journey at the foot of the cross. Have you made your decision to take up your cross and follow Jesus?

On a rocky hill outside Jerusalem long ago, three political prisoners were executed; but there was a vast difference between them. One died to sin, one died in sin, and One died for sin. Christ died for our sins. Now we must choose whether we will die in our sins or, by faith in Jesus, die to our sins.

THE LAST TOWER OF BABEL
CHAPTER THREE

An Amazing Fact: The Empire State Building in New York City was known for many years as the tallest building in the world. Completed in 1931, it stands 1,250 feet and boasts 102 stories of office space and more than 10 million bricks! Several structures in the world now surpass the Empire State Building in height, yet many of its construction records have never been broken. For example, because the building was made of prefabricated blocks, it was completed in less than two years. In fact, one 14-floor section was erected in less than a week!

The first time the word "kingdom" is found in the Bible, it is in connection with Babel (Genesis 10:8–10). The founder of that ancient city was Nimrod, a man whose very name means "we shall rebel." Throughout Scripture, Babel—which is the Hebrew word for "Babylon"—becomes a symbol of rebellion to God.

On the other hand, the first time the word "kingdom" appears in the New Testament, it is referring to God's kingdom. John the Baptist declared, *"Repent ye, for the kingdom of heaven is at hand"* (Matthew 3:2).

From cover to cover in the Bible, one can see a vivid contrast between these two opposing kingdoms, with the conflict reaching its culmination in the last book. In Revelation, the Babylonian kingdom is identified as the final power that will worship the beast and make war against God's people. To clearly understand these future events and this final struggle, we must first look back to the birth of Babel.

OLD BABYLON

"Now the whole earth had one language and one speech. And it came to pass, as they journeyed from the east, that they found a plain in the land of Shinar, and they dwelt there. Then they said to one another, 'Come, let us make bricks and bake them thoroughly.' They had brick for stone, and they had asphalt for mortar. And they said, 'Come, let us build ourselves a city, and a tower whose top is in the heavens; let us make a name for ourselves, lest we be scattered abroad over the face of the whole earth.' But the LORD came down to see the city and the tower which the sons of men had built. And the LORD said, 'Indeed the people are one and they all have one language, and this is what they begin to do; now nothing that they propose to do will be withheld from them. Come, let us go down and there confuse their language, that they may not understand one another's speech.' So the LORD scattered them abroad from there over the face of all the earth, and they ceased building the city. Therefore its name is called Babel, because there the LORD confused the language of all the earth; and from there the LORD scattered them abroad over the face of all the earth" (Genesis 11:1–9, NKJV).

Soon after the Flood, the human race began to rapidly multiply. In those days, men's lives were still measured by centuries, so many were born and few died. After only a few brief generations, thousands of descendants of Noah and his sons were swarming around the foothills of Ararat.

Evidently, Nimrod and some of the patriarchs suggested that they explore the region between the Tigris and Euphrates rivers, which had once been occupied by the garden of God. As they journeyed from the east, they were attracted to the lush climate and fertile soil in the plain of Shinar. Nimrod and the leaders believed their safety, strength and power would be in their numbers. So to prevent the people from diffusing around the world, they devised a plan to create a capital city for the planet and to centralize power in a new metropolis. Furthermore, they planned to inaugurate a new form of religion with a tower reaching to the heavens at the center of their kingdom.

Before the Flood, the patriarchs presented their sacrificial offerings to the Lord at the entrance of the Garden of Eden. But it is believed that God, to preserve Eden from destruction, raptured it up to heaven before the Flood. First, Revelation tells us that the tree of life, which was in the midst of the garden (Genesis 2:9), is still intact in the New Jerusalem (Revelation 2:7; 22:2). Second, it makes sense that if God can bring the New Jerusalem down from heaven at the end of this world, He could also have taken Eden up to heaven at the beginning of time. In any event, the builders of Babel decided, without consulting God, to dedicate this tower as the new place of worship and sacrifice.

SUN WORSHIP

K eep in mind that prior to the Flood, it never rained, and the sky had a different visual appearance. An even layer of moisture surrounded the planet, which polarized the rays of the sun and provided a uniform, mild temperature all around the world. This is why today we find thousands of tropical fern fossils in the freezing Polar Regions. Genesis 1:7 records, *"And God made the firmament, and divided the waters which were under the firmament from the waters which were above the firmament: and it was so."*

The Bible says that when the Flood came, *"the windows of heaven were opened"* (Genesis 7:11).

The first rainbow was one of many evidences that the Flood had drastically changed the earth. For the first time in history, man could look directly into the blazing glory of the sun and feel its burning power. People recognized that the sun had helped to dry the earth after the Flood and bring back the vegetation. So instead of worshiping the God who made the sun, the builders of Babel now considered the sun as an object of worship itself.

Today, all around the world, we can see towers, pyramids and ziggurats (step-towers) with altars dedicated to sun worship that can no doubt be traced back to Babel.

DETERMINED BUILDERS

A s much as scholars can tell, it is believed that construction on the tower of Babel ceased about 100 years after the Flood, or approximately 2200 BC. This date is based on Genesis 10:25, which says, *"Unto Eber were born two sons: the name of one was Peleg; for in his days was the earth divided."* This means that around the time Peleg was born, the union of Babel was divided and the tribes that would later grow into the nations of the world were dispersed. (The number of years between the Flood and the birth of Peleg is given in Genesis 11:10–16.)

Because the righteous Noah lived for another 350 years after the Flood, and Shem for 502 years after, it is safe to assume that not everyone alive at the time was in favor of the plans for a city and tower of Babel. The followers of God believed His promise that *"the waters shall no more become a flood to destroy all flesh"* (Genesis 9:15).

But the builders of Babel charged that God could not be trusted. Quite likely, those who advised against the project were severely ridiculed, persecuted, and made to appear as legalistic enemies of the common good. But in spite of their objections, the plan was agreed upon and building commenced.

The Flood's deluge had actually provided a new construction material. Bitumen tar, or asphalt, was in abundance after the distillation of massive peat fields, forests and other organic materials covered by sediment during the Flood. In addition, clay that could be baked into enduring bricks was also suddenly in great supply. Many hands make short work, and soon the massive tower began to rise toward the heavens. God is very patient and longsuffering, but there is a limit to His forbearance. Genesis 11:5 says, *"And the LORD came down to see the city and the tower, which the children of men builded."* This passage does not mean that God was unaware of the tower before He came down. Rather, this expression is the old Hebrew way of saying that God was ready to take action. The Lord uses the same phrase just before destroying Sodom (Genesis 18:21). God waited until the project was nearly completed, then He came down and took action.

Because of the tower's mounting height, it became necessary for the builders to transfer messages and orders for materials up and down its lofty walls with a relay system. But one day, without warning, the unbroken progress was abruptly halted. A mason called for a load of bricks but received a basket of straw instead. As the day wore on, the chaotic phenomena grew worse until the workers could no longer understand one another's speech.

As one writer puts it: "The builders were wholly unable to account for the strange misunderstandings among them, and in their rage and disappointment they reproached one another. Their confederacy ended in strife and bloodshed. Lightnings from heaven, as an evidence of God's displeasure, broke off the upper portion of the tower and cast it to the ground. Men were made to feel that there is a God who ruleth in the heavens."[1]

In humiliation and dismay, people began to band together in small groups that could comprehend one another's speech. Gradually, these groups migrated away from the doomed project and dispersed throughout the world. The babblings of Babel formed the parent languages of the earth, from which all other languages and dialects (now totaling more than 3,000) have developed.

The Hebrew word for Babel and Babylon is "babel" (pronounced baw-bel'), meaning confusion. It is from this word that we get the modern term "babbling." In Revelation, Babylon is a symbol for spiritual confusion. Some might be thinking, "Doesn't the Bible teach that God is not the author of confusion?" It is true that God's Spirit will never bring confusion into His worship (1 Corinthians 14:33), but there are many examples in Scripture where God has confused those who fight against Him (2 Kings 6:18; 7:6; 1 Corinthians 1:27).

THE OLD TOWER'S HISTORY

According to ancient history, there were several attempts in the next 1,400 years to repair the ruins of the tower. The last major effort was by Nebuchadnezzar II, who said that he received a command from his god Marduk to build it so that "its top might rival heaven." He called his temple tower, which stood in the sacred compound of the Marduk temple, Etemenanki, meaning "the foundation stone of heaven and earth." The ancient historian Herodotus wrote in 440 BC, "The tower of Babel was a furlong, or 660 feet, in length and breadth." According to the Greek historian Strabo, it rose to the same height, making it more than 200 feet taller than the great pyramid of Khufu.

The tower of Babel was likewise a pyramidal form, consisting of eight square towers, gradually decreasing in breadth. A winding ascent along the outside was broad enough to allow horses and carriages to pass each other, and even to turn around. At the apex was an altar where sacrifices were offered to the sun god.

The Persian king Xerxes later destroyed this infamous monument to rebellion. After Alexander the Great conquered the Persians, he too planned to rebuild the tower. In fact, most of the debris had been removed in preparation for its reconstruction when death suddenly took him.

Some have mistakenly thought that the references to Babylon in the New Testament prove that old Babylon will someday be rebuilt. In reality, the prophecies in Revelation regarding Babylon refer not to the literal kingdom by the Euphrates River, but rather to modern or spiritual Babylon. The Lord plainly foretold that ancient Babylon would be utterly destroyed and never rebuilt. *"And Babylon, the glory of kingdoms, the beauty of the Chaldees' excellency, shall be as when God overthrew Sodom and Gomorrah. It shall never be inhabited, neither shall it be dwelt in from generation to generation: neither shall the Arabian pitch tent there; neither shall the shepherds make their fold there"* (Isaiah 13:19, 20).

It is true that under the direction of Iraqi dictator Saddam Hussein, archeologists restored some of the ruins for tourists to view, but this in no way contradicts Isaiah's prophecy. In fact, Saddam had extensive plans to rebuild portions of the city for habitation to defy the Jewish prophecy. However, his plans had to be abandoned due to the Gulf War and the following economic sanctions, thus ratifying God's Word.

A MONUMENT TO FALSE RELIGIONS

There are at least six ways in which the tower of Babel is a pattern for all succeeding man-made religions:

1. **The tower was a monument to salvation by works.** The people who built the tower were not atheists; their great-grandparents had survived the Flood just 100 years before! So their basic plan was to build a tower from earth to heaven, and they labored under the pretense of wanting to be closer to God. The devil designed that this tower should be a subtle substitute for Jesus, who is the ladder from heaven to earth (John 1:51). Every false religion has in its root the error of Babel—that man can save himself by working from earth upward. But in reality, salvation is the result of God's initiative. John 3:16 says, *"For God so loved the world, that he gave his only begotten Son."* And in Ephesians 2:8, 9, the Bible declares: *"For by grace are ye saved through faith; and that not of yourselves: it is the gift of God: Not of works, lest any man should boast."*

2. **It was a monument to human pride.** The primary objective for the true Christian should be to bring glory to God's name. Jesus told His disciples, *"After this manner therefore pray ye: Our Father which art in heaven, Hallowed be thy name"* (Matthew 6:9). In contrast, the people's declared purpose for the tower was *"let us make a name for ourselves"* (Genesis 11:4, NKJV).

Interestingly, the word "denomination" means to unite under a name, and we know that many church denominations were brought into existence so leaders could "make a name" for themselves. The Bible tells us, *"Pride goeth before destruction, and an haughty spirit before a fall"* (Proverbs 16:18). Pride was where both the devil and the Babel builders fell.

3. **It was a monument to mankind's disobedience and defiance of God's will.** Immediately after the Flood, *"God blessed Noah and his sons, and said unto them, Be fruitful, and multiply, and replenish the earth"* (Genesis 9:1). They had clearly been commanded to disperse throughout the world and repopulate the earth, thus the confederacy at Babel was founded in rebellion to God's specific command. The people believed that there was strength in numbers and resisted God's plan because it would have weakened their power. God had placed the first family in a garden, but the Babel builders, like Cain (Genesis 4:17), chose to build a city. Like many today, they did not believe that God is very particular regarding obedience.

4. **It was a monument to human achievement.** The wisdom, technology, and techniques employed in the construction of this colossal edifice were state of the art for the day. When completed, it was hoped the majestic tower would be dazzling to behold and thus bring glory and attention to the designers and engineers. In other words, they sought to direct people's attention away from God's creation to the works of man. Even today, many are willing to overlook the false teachings and glaring inconsistencies of a religion because they are attracted to the magnificent temples, churches and cathedrals that house them.

5. **It was a monument to disbelief in God and His Word.** God had given a clear, binding covenant and had sealed it with a rainbow, saying, *"The waters shall no more become a flood to destroy all flesh"* (Genesis 9:15). But the Babel builders doubted God's Word. One objective in the tower's construction was to build higher than the Flood's water level and provide a retreat in the event that God would renege on His promise. Rather than trusting God to protect, provide and preserve them, they put their trust in a tower, in Nimrod, and in city walls.

6. **It was a monument to heaven on earth.** Time and time again, man has sought to create a kingdom on earth that does away with God and the need to turn from sin. By the time of Nebuchadnezzar, the city of Babylon had grown into a full-blown earthly counterfeit for God's New Jerusalem. It had great walls, a square design, hanging gardens in the center to mimic Eden's glory, a dazzling abundance of gold, and an immense river flowing through its center. Babel (and later Babylon) was mankind's feeble attempt to duplicate heaven and enjoy the New Jerusalem on earth without forsaking its sins.

In contrast, God's children *"looked for a city which hath foundations, whose builder and maker is God"* (Hebrews 11:10).

THE LAST TOWER OF BABEL

At Babel, God confused man's language so the people could not unite in their rebellion against Him. In these last days, the devil is using every means possible to once again unite humans in this rebellion. The information superhighway, high-speed travel and instant communication are all helping to lay the foundation for this final tower to man's unholy glory.

The Bible predicts that at the end, we will see more and more natural disasters, moral decay and economic and political turmoil. Just as men tried to save themselves from God's judgment at the tower of Babel, they will again unite at the end in an attempt to escape the final judgments from God.

Revelation speaks of this new Babylon as a threefold union that will unite to form the world's final stronghold of man-made religion. The apostle John writes: *"And I saw three unclean spirits like frogs coming out of the mouth of the dragon, and out of the mouth of the beast, and out of the mouth of the false prophet. For they are the spirits of devils, working miracles, which go forth unto the kings of the earth and of the whole world, to gather them to the battle of that great day of God Almighty"* (Revelation 16:13, 14).

These powers represent the great churches of the world, coming together to rally the nations for a common cause. Catholic, Protestant, charismatic and other churches will unite on major issues, but not based on those truths found in the Scriptures.

For those who think this could never happen, keep in mind the following sobering facts:

- Jesus said to His disciples (including you and me), *"the time cometh, that whosoever killeth you will think that he doeth God service"* (John 16:2).

- While Christ was on earth, His disciples and followers were all faithful church members, but so were the Jewish leaders who killed Him! Furthermore, it was one of His closest companions who betrayed Jesus into their hands.

- The churches of the world are already uniting! Every day, we hear another group claiming doctrines are no longer important as long as we agree on a few basic things. Look at how mainline Protestant churches have grasped the hand of Catholicism to "fight for the common good" on issues such as abortion and crime. Yes, these issues need to be dealt with, but not at the expense of Bible teachings.

At first, this threefold alliance will use pious, convincing arguments to urge all to join their movement and work together. Next, economic sanctions will be leveled against those who do not comply. *"That no man might buy or sell save he that had the mark, or the name of the beast, or the number of his name"* (Revelation 13:17). All will have to decide whether to obey the commandments of God or the laws of men. Most will be persuaded to compromise, but even the most severe measures won't shake the faithful from their solid foundation. Eventually, this religious-political power will set a date for the death penalty, *"and cause that as many as would not worship the image of the beast should be killed"* (Revelation 13:15).

But as in the days of Esther, when a decree was made to exterminate God's faithful people, He will once again confound their plans at the last moment and turn the tables on the wicked. Just before Jesus comes, those who have rebelled against the Lord will turn on one another as they did at Babel, and their union will dissolve in strife. Revelation 16:19 says, *"Now the great city was divided into three parts, and the cities of the nations fell: and great Babylon came in remembrance before God."*

Out of Babylon

With the imminent collapse and ruin of spiritual Babylon just ahead, we should not be surprised that God gives such a passionate appeal to those who are in danger of being destroyed along with it. Revelation 18:2–4 proclaims: *"And he cried mightily with a strong voice, saying, Babylon the great is fallen, is fallen. ... And I heard another voice from heaven, saying, Come out of her, my people, that ye be not partakers of her sins, and that ye receive not of her plagues."*

A great number of God's true followers are still in the communion of the churches that have been doctrinally deceived by Babel. Jesus said, *"And other sheep I have, which are not of this fold: them also I must bring, and they shall hear my voice; and there shall be one fold, and one shepherd"* (John 10:16).

A fascinating parallel to this calling-out process also took place in the days of the Old Testament. First, Abraham brought his wife Sarah out of Mesopotamia (the region of Babylon) and to the Promised Land. Then later, to find a wife for Isaac, Abraham's servant crossed the Euphrates to bring Rebekah out of the land of Babylon. And much later, God called His people out of Babylon to the land of Israel after 70 years of captivity (Jeremiah 29:10)!

Even more so today, God longs to bring His people out of the confusing, counterfeit religions of spiritual Babylon and into the truth of Canaan. The Bible makes it clear that in the last days, there will be only two groups of people. Those who remain in spiritual Babylon will follow the beast, receive its mark, and finally be destroyed. The others are the faithful, who keep the commandments of God, receive the seal of God, and follow the Lamb to glory. Revelation 14:12 identifies the key characteristics of this second group: *"Here is the patience of the saints: here are they that keep the commandments of God, and the faith of Jesus."*

Living in Babylon can be convenient and comfortable, but only those who are willing to brave the opposition, deny self, and follow Jesus to the Promised Land will be spared from the final plagues that will fall on Babylon. The rewards of heaven will infinitely outweigh any sacrifice. I invite you to follow Him now.

Perhaps you are wondering where you stand. Refusing to be part of any church is just as dangerous as being in Babylon. If you are questioning the doctrinal foundation of your church and are hearing the Master say, *"Come out of her My people,"* but you don't know where to go, write Amazing Facts today. Ask for a free copy of our booklet Search for the True Church, which explains how to use the Bible to identify God's true people.

---

1. Patriarchs and Prophets, p. 120.

THE FACETS OF FAITH
CHAPTER FOUR

An Amazing Fact: A placebo pill is made from an inert substance, such as sugar or starch, which is substituted for medicine to placate a person with imagined illnesses or else used as a control to avoid potential bias when testing new drugs. Although individuals taking the placebo should experience none of the medicine's benefits or side effects, many test patients have reported dramatic improvements, based on their belief in what the tested drug would do for them. In fact, doctors have administered placebos to patients diagnosed with incurable illnesses in an attempt to induce a temporary—or sometimes even permanent—improvement based on their faith in the doctor or medicine.

In a 1955 study by Dr. Henry Knowles Beecher, 35 percent of more than 1,000 patients tested reported that their conditions improved after receiving placebos. Scientists are unable to fully explain this phenomenon, but one theory links the patient's faith in a cure with the release of brain chemicals that might help promote healing.

A friend of mine who knows how much I enjoy playing racquetball recently gave me a $200 racquet as a gift. I think he got it on sale for 75 percent off, but nevertheless I was looking forward to giving it a try. In fact, I thought, "I'm going to win for a change, because I've got this $200 space-age racquet."

Sure enough, I won all three games the next time we played. Afterward, as I was putting my racquet away, I discovered that I had grabbed the wrong racquet out of my bag. Evidently, I had put the old racquet inside the new racquet bag and didn't notice when I pulled it out and started playing! I had thought I was playing with a $200 racquet, so I played much better, but the entire time I had been using the same old, crooked $39 racquet I'd had before.

Needless to say, there is a lot of power in faith. Motivational speakers who get paid thousands of dollars a day to inspire sales employees of major corporations are well aware of this. They call it the "power of positive thinking," which is another way of saying that a person's strongly held beliefs can influence him to do extraordinary things.

The Bible also promises great things for those who have faith. In the New Testament, Paul says, *"For by grace are ye saved through faith"* (Ephesians 2:8). And Habakkuk 2:4 tells us that *"the just shall live by his faith."*

What type of faith is the Bible talking about in these verses? Does positive thinking save us? Is it enough to tell ourselves over and over again that we will be saved, until we eventually begin to believe that it is true?

God doesn't leave us to wonder. As we study His Word, we find that there is no special merit in possessing a belief that is mere mental assent. The apostle James calls this the faith of devils. In the early church, some people were claiming that all you needed to do to be saved was to say you believed that Jesus is the Christ. However, James told them that genuine faith is always productive. He said, *"Shew me thy faith without thy works, and I will shew thee my faith by my works. Thou believest that there is one God; thou doest well: the devils also believe, and tremble"* (James 2:18–19). The devil has seen God and has walked in heaven and heard the angels sing. Consequently, his belief in God is much stronger than yours or mine. But obviously, that's not the kind of saving faith that the Bible advocates.

On the other hand, we are not saved by faith in what we ourselves can do either. John 3:16 does not say, *"For God so loved the world that he gave his only begotten son that whosoever believes in himself should ... have everlasting life."* No, it's not faith in ourselves or even faith in the power of faith. We are saved by faith in Christ and what God can do in us through Him.

SUFFICIENT FAITH

The Bible speaks much about this saving faith. In fact, the word "faith" is mentioned 231 times in the Bible, with 229 of these occurring in the New Testament. As we explore some of the various facets of a saving faith, I trust we'll learn not only how to recognize it, but also how to nurture it in our own lives.

When Jesus came to this world, one thing He found was a serious lack of faith among His people. He asked His disciples,

"Wherefore, if God so clothe the grass of the field, which to day is, and to morrow is cast into the oven, shall he not much more clothe you, O ye of little faith?" (Matthew 6:30). That phrase *"O ye of little faith"* appears again and again as Christ talked to the multitudes. They had let the cares of this world, and their pre-conceived ideas of the Messiah, cloud their view of the real thing and limit their faith.

In fact, I've found only two instances in the Gospels where Jesus credited anyone with having great faith. The first was a Roman soldier who declared, *"Lord, I am not worthy that thou shouldest come under my roof: but speak the word only, and my servant shall be healed"* (Matthew 8:5–13). The second person was a woman from Canaan who begged Jesus to heal her daughter (Matthew 15:21–28). Interestingly, neither of these two people were members of "the church." They were Gentiles from the surrounding nations.

Even Christ's closest followers were not immune from chastisement for their "little faith." In Matthew 8:23–27, we find the story of Jesus and His disciples in a boat on the Sea of Galilee. A great storm blew in, and while the disciples panicked, Jesus slept with perfect trust in His Father.

How many of us would be afraid if we were out on the sea in a terrible squall, with the boat being swamped with waves? I can understand their feelings, because I have been on boats larger than theirs during storms, and it is not fun. When you're far from shore and it's cold and the sky is black and the waters dark, you start to feel very mortal, vulnerable and small—even if you're on a big boat.

When the disciples roused Jesus to explain their situation, they must have been surprised by His reply. He asked them, *"Why are ye fearful, O ye of little faith? Then he arose, and rebuked the winds and the sea; and there was a great calm"* (Matthew 8:26).

Christ often chastised the disciples for having little faith, which means that there's hope for us. Even with little faith, God can do much.

In fact, one of the most wonderful and reassuring verses in the Bible tells us precisely how much faith we need to accomplish God's will for our lives. In it, Jesus says, *"Verily I say unto you, If ye have faith as a grain of mustard seed, ye shall say unto this mountain, Remove hence to yonder place; and it shall remove; and nothing shall be impossible unto you"* (Matthew 17:20). A mustard seed is one of the smallest seeds, yet even that amount of real faith can move mountains!

GENUINE FAITH

Although Jesus always dealt patiently with those who had a little faith, He strongly reprimanded those who tried to cover up their lack of faith by putting on an outward show of piety. He rebuked the Jewish religious leaders seven times in Matthew 23 for their false pretenses. And in the Sermon on the Mount, He plainly stated that these men prayed, fasted and gave offerings merely because they were concerned about what other people thought of them. They were doing good deeds not because they had faith or wanted to please God, but because they wanted to be seen by men.

Manifestations of false faith are one of the greatest obstacles to the conversion of the world. Christians need to demonstrate the genuine, sincere faith that Paul describes in 1 Timothy 1:5: *"Now the purpose of the commandment is love from a pure heart, from a good conscience, and from sincere faith"* (NKJV). When we begin to demonstrate this genuine faith and start to utilize it, we'll see many more conversions to the truth. People want to see Christianity "with skin on it."

Jesus relates this genuine faith to the perfect trust of a child. In Mark 10:15, He says, *"Verily I say unto you, Whosoever shall not receive the kingdom of God as a little child, he shall not enter therein."* Again in Matthew 18:3, He states, *"Except ye be converted, and become as little children, ye shall not enter into the kingdom of heaven."*

What is it about the attitude of a child that Jesus found so important? If you've been around children much, you know that they are very trusting of the adults in their lives. I remember hearing a story about a father and his little girl who were walking past a large puddle. It was so flat that they could see the sky reflected in it perfectly. Wanting to keep his daughter out of the water, the father told her, "Don't step in there, or you'll fall into the sky." His method worked, and the little girl stayed out of the water.

God does not tell us fantastic stories to keep us out of trouble, but He does want us to trust Him even when we don't understand His methods.

Here's what Corrie ten Boom, an old lady with childlike faith, said: "If all things are possible with God, then all things are possible to him who believes in Him." We need to have that kind of faith.

CONFIDENT FAITH

A nother aspect of a genuine, saving faith is that it is confident. It believes with surety that God can do what He says. In Mark 11:22–23, *"Jesus answering saith unto them, Have faith in God. For verily I say unto you, That whosoever shall say unto this mountain, Be thou removed, and be thou cast into the sea; and shall not doubt in his heart, but shall believe that those things which he saith shall come to pass; he shall have whatsoever he saith."*

That is a pretty amazing passage. It is as if God has removed the fine print and given us a boundless promise. The Bible says in James 1:5–6 that when you pray, you should pray believing that God will honor your request. If you ask and pray in faith in accordance with God's will, you can expect what you're praying for to be done.

Joshua must have believed this promise when he fought the Amorites during the battle at Gilgal. Israel was winning the battle, but night was drawing near. *"Then spake Joshua to the LORD in the day when the LORD delivered up the Amorites before the children of Israel, and he said in the sight of Israel, Sun, stand thou still upon Gibeon; and thou, Moon, in the valley of Ajalon. And the sun stood still, and the moon stayed, until the people had avenged themselves upon their enemies. ... So the sun stood still in the midst of heaven, and hasted not to go down about a whole day. And there was no day like that before it or after it, that the LORD hearkened unto the voice of a man: for the LORD fought for Israel"* (Joshua 10:12–14).

I have often wondered what was going through Joshua's mind when he prayed that audacious prayer and said, *"Sun stand still; moon do not move."* Sometimes we are willing to pray only if we have at least a 75 percent chance of success. Can you imagine the faith Joshua must have had in his bosom when he uttered that prayer for the sun to stand still? How dare anybody pray that the earth stop turning on its axis? Joshua obviously had genuine, mountain-moving faith.

VICTORIOUS FAITH

W hen we believe that God will do what He says, we will also believe that He can give us a victorious spiritual experience. The Bible often represents our spiritual walk as a battle. Paul says in

1 Timothy 6:12 that we are to *"Fight the good fight of faith, lay hold on eternal life."* One of the most important elements in any battle strategy is to believe you can win. We all need this kind of fighting faith.

Before I was a Christian, boxing intrigued me. My brother and I had gloves, and we used to box a little bit when we were young. I also enjoyed watching boxing matches, and one thing I noticed was that before a big fight, the boxers would always express their utmost confidence that they would win. They knew that if they didn't fully believe they would win, they had already lost the fight.

You and I must likewise believe with humble confidence that we can win through Christ. We cannot be like the evil spies who brought back a bad report from the land of Canaan. After seeing the people of that land, they said, *"We are not able to conquer it. We're not able."* And do you know what? They weren't able. They died in the desert.

However, Joshua and Caleb believed in God and said, *"Let us go up at once, and possess it; for we are well able to overcome it"* (Numbers 13:30). Forty years later, these two faithful men were the only ones of Israel's entire original adult population who made it to the Promised Land—because they believed that with God they could be victorious!

We also need to understand the weapon that Christ has given us for our spiritual battles. Ephesians 6:17 tells us that we are to use *"the sword of the Spirit, which is the word of God."* To achieve victory in fighting that fight of faith, we are to utilize the double-edged sword of God's Word. When Jesus was tempted in the wilderness (Matthew 4), He met every trial of Satan with the words, *"It is written."*

Interestingly, the very same weapon that we use in the fight of faith also increases our own faith. Romans 10:17 says, *"Faith cometh by hearing, and hearing by the word of God."* So if you want to get more of that faith to fight the battle, you need to read the Word of God.

Now when you believe in Christ's power and fight with the right weapons, you can be truly victorious. Too many times we miss out on miracles in our own lives because we don't believe that God can help. The Bible says: *"For whatsoever is born of God overcometh the world: and this is the victory that overcometh the world, even our faith. Who is he that overcometh the world, but he that believeth that Jesus is the Son of God?"* (1 John 5:4–5). Jesus tells us that all things are possible when we believe. This is victorious faith.

PATIENT FAITH

Sometimes the most challenging test of our faith is when things don't move according to our plan or timetable. We get impatient with God and tired of waiting on His schedule. People sometimes ask God to answer a prayer, and while they believe when they initially ask, their faith dries up if the answer does not come quickly.

In Matthew 25:1–13, Christ tells the parable of 10 virgins waiting for a bridegroom. While he tarried, the light went out for five of the waiting women. However, Jesus said, *"He that endureth to the end shall be saved"* (Matthew 10:22).

I think that what the church has to fear now more than anything else is this period of delay in which we're living. Several stories in the Bible help to illustrate this. When Moses delayed his return from the mountaintop, the people lost faith. While Samuel tarried, Saul lost his faith (and ultimately the kingdom) because he didn't have sufficient patience. When Jesus was praying in the garden, the disciples went to sleep.

It's during these episodes of delay that our faith is really tested. That's why we need the kind of faith that is going to hang on, and we need to persistently pray that we'll endure—not just for a little while, but until the end. When Elijah was praying for the rain to come after three and a half years of famine, how long did he pray? Untill it rained.

Perhaps you've been praying for somebody you love and your faith has begun to evaporate. Don't give up. The Bible tells us that one of the most important facets of faith is a patient, enduring faith that will not let go (James 1:3). Maybe you've been struggling to find a job. Maybe you've been looking for a godly mate or a business partner. It doesn't matter what the situation might be. Keep praying.

I remember reading about George Mueller, who persistently prayed that the Lord would save his friends and family. One by one, they came to the Lord. He prayed for one friend for 50 years, and at the time of the interview, that person still had not come to the Lord. However, Mueller said that he knew God was going to answer his prayer. That statement revealed a lot of faith. Incidentally, the individual did give his heart to the Lord at Mueller's funeral.

No Reason to Fear

Methodist minister John Wesley was in the church for years yet was not converted. One day, he boarded a boat along with a number of primitive Moravian Christians. While out at sea, they encountered a terrible storm. All hands were on deck as the vessel reeled violently on the waves. Water was rushing in and the sails were ripping; yet these Moravian families stood peacefully singing hymns.

Wesley, who was clinging to the side of the ship, asked, "Aren't you afraid?"

One of the men replied, "No, I'm not afraid."

"Well," asked a perplexed Wesley, "aren't the women and the children afraid?"

The man said: "No. We're not afraid to die. Our lives are in God's hands."

At that point Wesley became convicted that he did not really have faith in God.

Christians who have genuine faith trust God, regardless of the external circumstances. They know they have nothing to be afraid of, because He's on the throne. Ask Christ to increase your faith today so that He can do even greater things in your life.

FINDING THE MISSING PEACE
CHAPTER FIVE

An Amazing Fact: Do you know the strange events that led to the prestigious Nobel Prize? Alfred Nobel invented "safety blasting powder"—better known as dynamite, which is five times more potent than gunpowder. It made construction with explosives safer, more efficient, and cheaper. But military leaders also realized the value of dynamite. However, the man known as the "Lord of Dynamite" was a pacifist and was greatly troubled by the wartime use of his inventions. In 1895, a newspaper mistakenly published Nobel's obituary while he lived! He was horrified to read that he'd be remembered as a man whose invention was linked to so much death and carnage. So upon his death, perhaps in an effort to alleviate his conscience and improve his legacy, Nobel's will provided that the bulk of his vast fortune go to a fund that would annually celebrate advancements in science, literature and peace.

"**B**ut the meek shall inherit the earth; and shall delight themselves in the abundance of peace" (Psalm 37:11).

PEACE FROM WITHIN

Everybody desires peace. Many are longing for political peace. Others are craving mental, financial, social and even physical peace. But most of the world seems to believe some external change in circumstances is what will bring lasting peace.

In Mark 4, we find the familiar story of Jesus sleeping through a storm. A great windstorm arose, and the waves beat into the boat, but Jesus was in the stern, asleep on a pillow. *"And he arose and rebuked the wind, and said unto the sea, Peace, be still. And the wind ceased, and there was a great calm."*

This is a fascinating tale, because the disciples wake Jesus to ask Him a very strange question: "Don't you care that we're perishing?"

Of course He cares—that's why He came to earth! Jesus said, *"God so loved the world … that they might not perish."*

Naturally, Christ was not distressed by the raging elements. In fact, He did not need to shout; rather, His words, spoken in faith, were potent enough. I imagine He might have even yawned, rubbed the sleep from His eyes, and stood to calmly survey the storm. I think He simply spoke, "Hush. Be quiet. Be at peace." With that, the wind instantly stopped and the waters instantaneously flattened to a glassy calm. That's the way it is with God; He can instantly soothe all our fears.

However, when the disciples were rescued from their fear, they were still "exceedingly" afraid. But why after the storm was gone? Now they are wondering, "What manner of man is this, that even the winds and the sea obey Him?" The elements had peace, but the disciples were still afraid. It's clear their absence of peace was beyond environmental. Something else took away their peace— something on the inside. They did not know Jesus.

Like the disciples, we become anxious and lose faith when the gale blows. We wonder, "Does God care?"

GOD IS PEACE

A while ago, I was frustrated with a series of problems I faced as a pastor and parent. I wasn't wringing my hands, but I did have many anxious moments. I woke up at night, my mind churning over this bundle of challenges. What bothered me most about this reaction was that I knew it demonstrated a lack of faith. I've learned so much more about peace since then, and I would like to pass on to you a few aspects of what the Lord taught me.

Some of the best advertising for Christ is to exude peace no matter the external circumstances. Not only is God love, but He is also the essence of peace. I went through the Bible and found seven times when God is identified as a God of Peace. We don't normally think of that as one of His titles, but it is—and I believe it is an important one. God does not bite His nails, nor does He pace the floor. God is never nervous, edgy or restless.

NOT JUST A WORD

The word "peace" is found about 430 times in the Bible, which means God has a lot to say about the importance of this theme. The Hebrew word for peace is shalom, which can be used to say "hello" or "goodbye." In essence, shalom means peace, safety, well-being, happy, friendly, healthy, prosperity and favor. The New Testament uses the Greek word "irane" for peace. This is where we get the name Irene. It can mean: peace, prosperity, one, quietness, rest, to set at one again, and to restore. Great words, aren't they? They are sweet, endearing words. And the entire plan of salvation revolves around these words because we are alienated from God; we are at war. And Jesus, who is the pure Prince of Peace, has come to reconcile us. He came to make peace with the Father on our behalf, because our sins have separated us from God.

TRUE PEACE

When people talk about peace, they say, "Let's pray for peace." What kind of peace do they mean? Usually, it's global or civil peace. But is this primarily why Jesus came?

Many fear nuclear war, so they ask for world peace so nations don't annihilate each other. Even with the current wave of disarmament, the nuclear nations still have enough weapons to exterminate life on this planet. And now an army of fanatical terrorists is trying to obtain nuclear weapons. That might leave you feeling a little edgy. If you didn't know that God was on His throne, you might never sleep!

What about political peace? Jesus warns, *"Think not that I am come to send peace on earth: I came not to send peace, but a sword"* (Matthew 10:34). Wars and crusades have been fought in Jesus' name, so this can't be the peace He's offering. Herbert Hoover said, "Peace is not made at the council tables, or by treaties, but in the hearts of men."

Some long for domestic peace, plagued by constant conflict in their homes—which have become battle zones. The Bible says it's bad for a woman to marry a lazy man. And for a man to be married to an irritable woman, *"It is better to dwell in the wilderness"* (Proverbs 21:19). And yet even this domestic peace is not the real reason Jesus came, because He said, *"For I am come to set a man at variance against his father, and the daughter against her mother, and the daughter-in-law against her mother-in-law"* (Matthew 10:35). The gospel of Christ can most certainly bring peace into a divided home, but it can just as easily bring division. Domestic tranquility is not why Jesus is called the Prince of Peace.

Still others seek peace through financial security. Every day they anxiously check the stocks, and if the market goes up, they're serene; but when it drops, they're agitated. Some are constantly fending off and stalling bill collectors. Who can have peace living like that? It's hard to have peace when you're daily drowning in debt. Some people think, "If I could just win the lottery, then I'd have peace." But the Bible says peace does not come from the abundance of things a man possesses. Proverbs 11:28 says, *"He that trusteth in his riches shall fall: but the righteous shall flourish as a branch."* No. Real peace does not come from financial security either.

FALSE PEACE

The devil wants us to pursue false peace through the popular counterfeits of finances, domestic affairs and the world in general. He even has some people looking for peace through cult-like religions or rituals, while persuading others to turn hopelessly to drugs for temporary sensations of peace.

Many are distracted and deceived by these false forms of peace. Ezekiel 13:10 says, *"They have seduced my people saying, Peace; and there was no peace."* Many politicians have greased their way into office by promising peace. Before Jerusalem was destroyed, the religious leaders told the people, "God is going to defend us." They claimed "Peace!" And they were destroyed. In Isaiah 57:21, we're warned, *"There is no peace, saith my God, to the wicked."* Though false prophets promise them peace, those without God won't find it.

In 1 Thessalonians 5:3, we read, *"For when they shall say Peace and safety; then sudden destruction cometh upon them as travail upon a woman with child; and they shall not escape."* We need to especially be concerned when we hear world leaders shouting, "Peace and safety are on the horizon." It is a popular platitude, but that's not the kind of peace God promises. All these conditional concepts of peace change so quickly. Remember Job? He lost his financial, physical and family serenity suddenly. But he did not lose his peace (Job 22:21). Conditions will always change, so we shouldn't be caught off guard by trusting in false peace. The devil can use these illusions to make us complacent and then he pulls the rug out from under us!

THE ENEMIES OF PEACE

So where do you find abiding peace that gives you rest no matter what your circumstances? "All men desire peace," someone said. "But few people desire those things that make for peace." Often those seeking peace insulate themselves against it by falling victim to its enemies—such as fear, greed, ambition, envy, anger and pride. Anyone embracing these traits can't have peace. They must let them go to make room for and nurture the peace of God. We cannot cling to pride or greed and then say, "God, grant me peace." Those enemies must first be evicted from the heart.

Peace is also something you'll miss by aiming directly for it. It's like happiness: If you spend your life trying to make yourself happy, you'll lose it (Matthew 16:25). You find happiness by serving and loving others. So if peace is something you're looking for in and of itself, you'll never experience it.

WHERE TO BEGIN

I'm amazed by the Bible story of Peter sleeping like a baby even while on death row. That's incredible! He had a peace that surpasses understanding. How would you like to find that kind of peace where you don't need to be anxious even though your life is on the line? Martin Luther said, "True peace is not merely the absence of some negative force. It is rather the presence of some positive force." Ridding yourself of negative forces will provide peace only temporarily. Eventually, some other crisis will sprout to displace your temporary tranquility—a constant roller coaster of peace and worry. True, abiding peace must be something more.

I once saw a bumper sticker that said, "No God, No peace; Know God, Know peace." I thought, "That's clever!" Because that's exactly where true peace comes from: knowing God. Job 22: 21 says, *"Acquaint now thyself with him, and be at peace."* How do we acquaint ourselves with God? Through communion; His Word. By allowing Him to speak to us, we'll find peace. And we are promised that when we pray, *"The peace of God, which passeth all understanding, shall keep your hearts and minds through Christ Jesus"* (Philippians 4:7). He'll give you this peace that surpasses understanding when you begin to know Him.

THE SOURCE

Thomas Jefferson once said, "When you start becoming anxious… count to 10. If that doesn't work, count to 10 again." That's quaint, sound advice; but the real power of peace is found in the promises of God's Word. Christ met every one of Satan's temptations with that Word. Knowing Scripture gave Jesus the power and peace to overcome. An attitude of gratitude can also become a source of peace. Focus on those things for which you should be grateful. Sometimes, we get agitated because we have forgotten our blessings and ponder our problems. We become discontent by focusing on what is wrong and forget everything that is right. Thank God for what you do have. Remember, Paul said, you pray, you supplicate, you request, and then you thank. After thanking God then the God of Peace will give you that incredible peace (Philippians 4:6, 7).

God will also guard your heart and mind through Jesus against the devil's attacks of distress, designed to destroy your peace. The strongest witness is when a Christian can demonstrate peace even when passing through trial. When you're peacefully going through a storm, you have a converting influence on others. David said, *"I will both lay me down in peace, and sleep: for thou, LORD, only makest me dwell in safety"* (Psalm 4:8). Even though King Saul and an entire army were hunting to kill him, David could sleep because he knew God was with him.

HAVE A PEACE SUMMIT

We need to have a peace conference with the Prince of Peace. Most people are centered in self, which is like trying to find peace at the epicenter of an earthquake. To have one's world centered in God is real peace. He's the calm in the eye of a hurricane. The storm might be raging around you, but within all is still. Peace also comes from meditation—and I'm not talking about transcendental meditation. Rather, the Bible tells us to meditate on God, which we can do in so many ways. At our mountain home, my family can see a beautiful valley cascading below. A friend built us a beautiful oak swing on the porch, and my wife spends much time there just meditating. One day, I began feeling restless because of mounting unfinished projects. But finally, I thought, "I need to try that!" So I joined her up on the swing. We gently rocked back and forth, and I surveyed the meadows and the birds. Then I heard that still, small voice. The Bible tells us to be still and to know that He is God. I found myself at peace.

Behold God's creation, and you'll find real rest. Isaiah 26:3 says, *"Thou wilt keep him in perfect peace, whose mind is stayed on thee: because he trusteth in thee."* This is true meditation: keeping your mind fixed on God. I like to call this condition a "calm-plex." And when you stay your mind on God, you can have that calm-plex.

CONNECTING THE PEACES

I saw a sign in front of a church that said, "If life is a puzzle, look here for the missing peace." It suggests that along with reading the Word, meditation, prayer and trust, you need to learn about that missing peace in the church environment. Peace can be contagious. We learn much about the peace of God by fellowship with others who know the Prince of Peace.

Peace also comes from obedience—by knowing you're in God's will and surrendering to Him. Philippians 4:9 says, *"Those things, which ye have both learned, and received, and heard, and seen in me, do: and the God of peace shall be with you."* That's an important biblical message. *"Mark the perfect man, and behold the upright: for the end of that man is peace"* (Psalm 37:37). Many people haven't associated peace with obedience, but the Bible is clear: *"Great peace have they which love thy law: and nothing shall offend them"* (Psalm 119:165).

In fact, when I counsel a fretful soul, I usually ask, "Is there something you're doing that is not in harmony with God's will?" Often they'll admit to being disobedient in some area. Would you want your children to be at peace if they were disobeying you?

Likewise, God loves you too much to let you have peace when you are disobeying your conscience and His will.

Jonah is a great example of this—running west when God said go east. He soon found himself in the storm, having lost his peace when he went directly against the will of God. The Bible is full of similar stories that remind us of this principle. *"The work of righteousness shall be peace; and the effect of righteousness quietness and assurance forever"* (Isaiah 32:17).

Peace Is a River

Isaiah 48:18 says, *"O that thou hadst hearkened to my [commands]! then had thy peace been as a river."* Isaiah doesn't say, "Your peace would have been like a creek." Do you know why? A creek dries up. But a river doesn't; it is continual. (Rivers may fall or rise some, but they always flow.) It's constant, just like peace. It just keeps on moving—it's always there, available, and ever flowing.

Erwin Lutzer said, "Emotional peace and calm come after doing God's will, and not before." I once stole from my employer when I was 15 years old. I never forgot. It wasn't much money, but years later, after I was born-again, the Holy Spirit said, "Doug, you need to go and pay them back." I didn't want to, and so I lost my peace. I tried to explain my conscience away, "Oh, that was 20 years ago and such a little amount." I had accepted Christ, and God had forgiven me—so why was it bothering me?

I think it has to do with progressive peace. To stay at peace means you must continually walk in God's will as He reveals things… always flowing forward. Many Christians have new truths revealed to them but say, "I don't want to walk like that because it's different." And sure enough, they lose their peace! If God reveals new light, you can't refuse to walk in it. The Lord finally graced me with strength, and I returned to the place where I once worked. I went in, my hands sweating. Ironically, the employer I stole from was no longer there and no one knew where he went. But I found peace. You see, God didn't want my $15. He wanted my willingness to make things right. And once I was in God's will for me, I had my peace back again. I was a river once more. "When peace, like a river attendeth my way, it is well with my soul."

PEACEMAKERS

God has called you to be at peace, but He also wants you to be a peacemaker. He wants you to share that peace with others. Don't keep it to yourself because, like happiness, it's something you retain by giving it away. Jesus said, *"Blessed are the peacemakers: for they shall be called the children of God"* (Matthew 5:9).

How are we to be peacemakers? Are we to become politicians with a seat at the United Nations? Not particularly. As Christian peacemakers, we are to invite people to make peace with their God. That's the foremost responsibility. In Luke 10:5, Jesus sends out His apostles to preach. He instructs them to say *"Peace be to this house"* when they entered a new home.

And we are to give this benediction to a world in turmoil. As we invite the Prince of Peace into our hearts, we are then called to communicate Him to an anxious and fretful world.

When the priests would bless the people, they would say, *"The* LORD *bless thee, and keep thee; The* LORD *make his face to shine upon thee, And be gracious to thee. The* LORD *lift up His countenance upon thee, And give thee peace"* (Numbers 6:24–26). We are a nation of priests. Christ came to bring us peace, so He sends us to bring other people peace.

THE ROCK

Do you want to find peace? Jesus, the Prince of Peace, is the missing piece. The gospel opens with an angel singing, *"Peace and goodwill toward men."* Christ entered the world with a proclamation of peace. And He concluded His ministry the same way. Before ascending to heaven, He appears to His disciples in the upper room and says, *"Peace be unto you."* And He repeats this for them again and again. This is why He's called the Prince of Peace. Ephesians 2:14–17 says this about our King: *"For He Himself is our peace, who has made both one, and has broken down the middle wall of separation ... thus making peace [and] putting to death the enmity. And He came and preached peace to you who are afar off, and to those who are near"* (NKJV). We are at war with God. But Jesus unites us. Jesus brings peace between the Father and us.

A few years ago, my wife Karen and I went scuba diving at the

Great Barrier Reef. We got caught in a storm on this small charter boat. The captain said our lives were at risk and whatever we paid didn't matter. He then steered the boat behind a huge rock near an island. And as we were anchored behind that rock, the storm raged around us—but that night, we were sheltered from the wet gale by this island rock, and we slept peacefully. During the night, the anchor slipped and we were rocked awake violently. But the captain simply got up and steered us back behind the rock. It was soon calm once more.

Jesus is our Rock. The world is full of storms, and we'll find true shelter only under His wings. *"Peace I leave with you,"* Jesus says. *"My peace I give unto you: not as the world giveth ... unto you"* (John 14:27). God wants you to have peace! It's not political, social, physical, domestic, or financial peace. It's an internal peace that God gives, not like the world gives. It's a peace like a river, a peace that passes understanding.

PEACE, PERFECT PEACE

In the world, you're going to have tribulation, but be of good cheer, because Jesus has overcome the world for you. Christ said that no matter what is happening in the world, you can have peace. *"These things I have spoken unto you, that in me ye might have peace"* (John 16:33). Jesus is the best example of peace; He didn't allow outward circumstances destroy His inner peace with the Father. He is the epitome of peace—the very essence. His peace wasn't contingent on physical relief from hunger or torture; rather, it sprang from a deep internal well. It wasn't reliant on His finances or social acceptance. His own people forsook Him, but He still had peace. It wasn't conditional on domestic bliss either, as His own family misunderstood Him.

Jesus' peace was such that He withstood the test of everything the world and the devil threw at Him. All the legions of hell assailed Him to take away His peace, and they couldn't touch it because it was hidden in God. I want you to have that kind of peace—a peace that no devil can rob. If you want it, you can have it through a trusting relationship with God, communion in prayer, fellowship with His people, and through building on His Word.

Now you know the source of true peace in this life, but a more perfect peace is surely to come. Someday, there will be nothing but total peace everywhere. Isaiah 11:6 promises *"The wolf also shall dwell with the lamb, and the leopard shall lie down with the kid; and the calf and the young lion ... and a little child shall lead them."* This means peace in creation, peace in our relationships, peace in the whole world. The promise is simply waiting for the peacemakers to claim it.

Fig Leaves and Pharisees
Chapter Six

You've probably heard the expression "face the music." But you might not know that it is believed to have originated in Japan.

According to the story, the imperial orchestra once humored a man who couldn't play a note. Because of his wealth and great influence, the man demanded that a seat be given to him in the group because he wanted to "perform" before the emperor. The conductor agreed to let him sit in the second row of the orchestra and hold a flute, even though the man couldn't read a dot of music. As a concert would begin, he'd simply raise his instrument, pucker his lips, and move his fingers. He went through all the motions of playing, but never made a sound. This deception continued for two years.

However, a new conductor took over when the old one retired. He told the orchestra members that he wanted to audition each player personally. One by one, they performed in his presence. Then came the phony flutist's turn. He was frantic with worry, so he pretended to be sick. However, a doctor ordered to examine him declared that he was perfectly well. The new conductor insisted that the man appear and demonstrate his skill. Shamefacedly, the phony had to confess that he was a fake. He wanted the prestige of being part of the orchestra, but since he never took the time to learn his instrument, he was unable to "face the music."

The word "hypocrite" comes from the Greek word "hupokrites." It is defined as "the practice of professing beliefs, feelings, or virtues that one does not hold or possess" or "an actor under an assumed character."

Someone said, "The number one cause of atheism is Christians. Those who proclaim God with their mouths and deny Him with their lifestyles are what an unbelieving world finds simply unbelievable." [1] And Oswald Chambers said, "The world is glad of an excuse not to listen to the gospel message, and the inconsistencies of Christians is the excuse." [2]

MAN-MADE COVERUP

The Lord hates hypocrisy. Jesus made this painfully clear in His sermon on the mount. He told the people, *"Take heed that ye do not your alms [charitable deeds] before men, to be seen of them: otherwise ye have no reward of your Father which is in heaven. Therefore when thou doest thine alms, do not sound a trumpet before thee, as the hypocrites do in the synagogues and in the streets, that they may have **glory of men**"* (Matthew 6:1, 2, emphasis added).

He continued, *"And when thou prayest, thou shalt not be as the hypocrites are: for they love to pray standing in the synagogues and in the corners of the streets, that they may be **seen of men**. Moreover when ye fast, be not, as the hypocrites, of a sad countenance: for they disfigure their faces, that they may **appear unto men** to fast"* (verses 15, 16, emphasis added).

The Pharisees were experts in the art of faking true religion. They fasted, prayed, and gave to be *"seen of men."*

Now I said that the Lord hates hypocrisy, and it's true. But thank God that He loves the hypocrites, or we would all be in trouble! Arthur R. Adams said, "Don't stay away from church because there are so many hypocrites. There's always room for one more."

The famous actor Robert Redford was walking through a hotel lobby one day, and a fan followed him to the elevator. "Are you the real Robert Redford?" she asked with great excitement. As the doors of the elevator closed, he replied, "Only when I am alone!"

If truly honest, we would all admit that at times we manufacture feelings and attitudes that are less than genuine—a "public relations" image. In fact, we can see that from the very beginning of this world's history, hypocrisy has been man's feeble way of cloaking sin.

The Bible records: *"When the woman saw that the tree was good for food, and that it was pleasant to the eyes, and a tree to be desired to make one wise, she took of the fruit thereof, and did eat, and gave also unto her husband with her; and he did eat. And the eyes of them both were opened, and they knew that they were naked; and they sewed fig leaves together, and made themselves aprons"* (Genesis 3:6, 7).

Keep in mind that before sin, Adam and Eve were not streaking around the garden of Eden in their birthday tuxedos. In the garden, man had the privilege of talking with God face to face. Thus he was clothed with an aura of light—the same type of light that shone from Moses' face after he spent time in the presence of God (Exodus 34:29–35). But after Adam and Eve sinned, the light went out and they sensed their nakedness.

Notice that their first reaction to sin was to manufacture a cover-up. When they lost their garments of light as a result of disobedience, Adam and Eve used fig leaves to cover their shame. Before sin, they had never seen anything die, so when they plucked the fig leaves from the tree, I'm sure they expected longer-lasting results. When I picked some fig leaves, I was amazed how quickly they became limp and shriveled. In addition, I found their pungent odor offensive. How very sad that our first parents traded living robes of light for limp, stinky leaves that soon withered and died.

When God spoke to Adam and Eve, He explained that to cover their sin, something besides fig leaves would have to die. At this point, God established the sacrificial system. *"Unto Adam also and to his wife did the LORD God make coats of skins, and clothed them"* (Genesis 3:21). Adam and Eve made skimpy belts of fig leaves, but God gave them robes of skin, thus symbolizing that Jesus would have to die to cover the sin and nakedness of the lost.

When we sin, one of two things will happen. We either start looking for fig leaves to make our own flimsy cover-up, or we look to Jesus for His robe of righteousness.

MERELY ORNAMENTAL

Throughout the Bible, fig leaves are a symbol for man-made religion and false righteousness. The fig tree is a symbol of God's people.

Please read the following passage carefully: *"He spake also this parable; A certain man had a fig tree planted in his vineyard; and he came and sought fruit thereon, and found none. Then said he unto the dresser of his vineyard, Behold, these three years I come seeking fruit on this fig tree, and find none: cut it down; why cumbereth it the ground? And he answering said unto him, Lord, let it alone this year also, till I shall dig about it, and dung it: And if it bear fruit, well: and if not, then after that thou shalt cut it down"* (Luke 13:6–9).

Year after year, the owner of the vineyard was disappointed because all he found on his fig tree was leaves. It bore no fruit. It looked like a healthy tree, but he did not plant it for mere ornamental beauty. He wanted fruit.

I believe there also may be a time prophecy hidden in this parable. The vineyard mentioned in verse 6 is the land of Israel (Isaiah 5:1–7; Jeremiah 12:10; Psalm 80:8–16), in which the vine and fig tree—both symbols of Israel and Judah—were planted. The parable of the fig tree gives a total of four years from the time of planting to the final chance for the tree to bear fruit. Now a year in the Bible is 360 days, because the Jews operated on a lunar calendar. Four years would be a total of 1,440 days. A day in prophecy equals a year (Numbers 14:34; Ezekiel 4:6). According to many chronologists, Joshua crossed over the Jordan and took possession of the Promised Land at approximately 1407 BC. If you extend 1,440 years from that point in time (keeping in mind that there is no zero year), you come to the year AD 34. This important date in history is the same ending point for the 490-year prophecy given in Daniel 9:24. The angel says, *"Seventy weeks are determined upon thy people and upon thy holy city,"* and in fact the word "determined" is better translated as "cut off." The parable of the fig tree said, *"Then after that thou shalt cut it down"* (Luke 13:9, emphasis added). It was in AD 34 that the Jews forfeited their place as God's covenant people. Then in AD 70, both Jerusalem and the temple were completely destroyed.

MISSING FRUIT

One week before His death, Jesus cursed a fruitless fig tree to illustrate what was going to happen to the Jewish nation and the apostate church.

"Now in the morning as he returned into the city, he hungered. And when he saw a fig tree in the way, he came to it, and found nothing thereon, but leaves only, and said unto it, Let no fruit grow on thee henceforward for ever. And presently the fig tree withered away. And when the disciples saw it, they marvelled, saying, How soon is the fig tree withered away!" (Matthew 21:18–20).

Why did Jesus curse a fig tree? Surely the Lord was not so petty as to retaliate against a tree because it didn't give Him breakfast! We need to examine this story closely, because it is the only place in the Gospels where Jesus is credited with being directly responsible for killing something.

Fig trees are unique in that both mature leaves and ripe fruit appear at the same time. The tree Jesus cursed had all the outward signs of bearing fruit, yet the tree was a hypocrite. It was a fitting symbol of the Jewish nation. With its temple, priesthood, and sacrifices, Israel had all the trappings of true religion, but the genuine fruits—justice, mercy and faith (Matthew 23:23)—were missing. Remember that withered fig leaves are a reminder of man's failed attempts to cover his own sins.

Notice the sequence: The same day Jesus cursed the fruitless fig tree (Matthew 21), He later had a showdown with the phony Pharisees and exposed their hypocrisy. *"But all their works they do for to be seen of men"* (Matthew 23:5). Seven times Jesus called them hypocrites, and then He pronounced a curse on them—just as He had the fig tree earlier that day. Here is the curse: *"Wherefore, behold, I send unto you prophets, and wise men, and scribes: and some of them ye shall kill and crucify; and some of them shall ye scourge in your synagogues, and persecute them from city to city: That upon you may come all the righteous blood shed upon the earth, from the blood of righteous Abel unto the blood of Zacharias son of Barachias, whom ye slew between the temple and the altar. Verily I say unto you, All these things shall come upon this generation"* (Matthew 23:34-36). Please don't miss the fact that Jesus said the curse would *"come upon this generation."*

In the next chapter, when Jesus describes the destruction of Jerusalem and the end of the world, He gives fig leaves as a sign. *"Now learn a parable of the fig tree; When his branch is yet tender, and putteth forth leaves, ye know that summer is nigh: So likewise ye, when ye shall see all these things, know that it is near, even at the doors. Verily I say unto you, This generation shall not pass, till all these things be fulfilled"* (Matthew 24:32–35).

A generation in the Bible is 40 years (Numbers 32:13). Jesus made this prophecy in AD 31, and by AD 70 it was fulfilled!

Christ's illustration of the fig tree that put forth leaves but no fruit is also a very plain prophetic sign for the last days. In the same way that literal Israel had all the outward forms of true religion before the destruction of Jerusalem in AD 70, so spiritual Israel (the church) in the last days will put forth leaves but no fruit. There might be all the outward appearances of revival—lots of praise, miracle-healing services, big attendance, and talk of love and acceptance, but no fruit of the Holy Spirit. In other words, *"having a form of godliness, but denying the power thereof"* (2 Timothy 3:5).

One of my favorite Christian authors made a clear prediction more than 100 years ago: "Before the final visitation of God's judgments upon the earth there will be among the people of the Lord such a revival of primitive godliness as has not been witnessed since apostolic times. The Spirit and power of God will be poured out upon His children. At that time many will separate themselves from those churches in which the love of this world has supplanted love for God and His word. Many, both of ministers and people, will gladly accept those great truths which God has caused to be proclaimed at this time to prepare a people for the Lord's second coming. The enemy of souls desires to hinder this work; and before the time for such a movement shall come, he will endeavor to prevent it by introducing a counterfeit. In those churches which he can bring under his deceptive power he will make it appear that God's special blessing is poured out; there will be manifest what is thought to be great religious interest. Multitudes will exult that God is working marvelously for them, when the work is that of another spirit. Under a religious guise, Satan will seek to extend his influence over the Christian world." [3]

This fig-leaf righteousness and false revival are the characteristics of the last-day Laodicean church. *"Because thou sayest, I am rich, and increased with goods, and have need of nothing [recognize the fig leaves?]; and knowest not that thou art wretched, and miserable, and poor, and blind, and naked: I counsel thee to buy of me gold tried in the fire, that thou mayest be rich; and white raiment, that thou mayest be clothed, and that the shame of thy nakedness do not appear; and anoint thine eyes with eyesalve, that thou mayest see. As many as I love, I rebuke and chasten: be zealous therefore, and repent"* (Revelation 3:17–19).

Jesus is calling us to lay aside our filthy, self-righteous fig leaves and—like the prodigal son—come home and put on the royal robe of the Father. Only then will the fruits of the Spirit, which are love, joy, peace, longsuffering, gentleness, goodness, faith, meekness, and temperance (Galatians 5:22, 23), be evident in our lives. There will be no people in God's kingdom who are merely ornamental trees. Everyone must have fruit.

"Let love be without hypocrisy" (Romans 12:9, NKJV). Hypocrisy hurts the church, and it hurts us. Many hypocrites have been acting

for so long that they have come to believe their own performances. We have a tendency to mold our faces to fit our masks. But God wants us to be honest with others and ourselves—spiritual Israelites in whom there is no guile or deceit (1 Peter 2:1; Revelation 14:5).

Here is the challenge I want to present to you: "The greatest want of the world is the want of men—men who will not be bought or sold, men who in their inmost souls are true and honest, men who do not fear to call sin by its right name, men whose conscience is as true to duty as the needle to the pole, men who will stand for the right though the heavens fall." [4]

Jesus says, *"Blessed are the pure in heart: for they shall see God"* (Matthew 5:8).

---

1. Karl Rahner, quoted in Draper's Book of Quotes for the Christian World, compiled by Edyth Draper (Wheaton: Tyndale House Publishers, Inc.), 1992, entry #487.

2. Ibid. Oswald Chambers, entry #1334.

3. E.G. White, The Great Controversy (Pacific Press Publishing Association: Mountain View, CA), 1950, p. 464, emphasis added.

4. E.G. White, Education, (Pacific Press Publishing Association: Mountain View, CA), 1952, p. 57.

A PERFECT CHRISTIAN?
CHAPTER SEVEN

An Amazing Fact: Bumblebees were originally called "humble bees" because they are generally good-natured and rarely sting. The young children of early settlers struggled to say "humble bees," and often called them "bumble bees" instead. Because of the awkward movements of the adult bees, the new name stuck.

Bumblebees are among the few insects that can control their body temperature. In cold weather, queens and workers can shiver their flight muscles to warm themselves. Their large size and heat-conserving hairy coats also help them stay warm, allowing them to work in colder climates and lower temperatures that most other insects like to avoid.

Aviation engineers have also studied bumblebees and determined that with their small wings and hairy, fat bodies, it is aerodynamically impossible for them to fly. But bumblebees ignore these reports and continue to fly.

As I write, I've been staying in a hotel for a few days. I tossed and turned last night trying unsuccessfully to acquire a good night's sleep in the hotel bed. In the process of thrashing around, I managed to twist up the sheets, exposing the mattress' product name: "Perfect Sleeper." Funny. I can't say I had a perfect night's sleep.

In such a perfectly imperfect world, most have come to accept that perfect does not always mean flawless. Yet Jesus said, *"Be ye therefore perfect, even as your Father which is in heaven is perfect"* (Matthew 5:48).

What does Jesus mean when He asks us to be perfect? After all, everyone echoes "nobody's perfect"—let alone perfect as our Father in heaven! This passage in Matthew has been an ongoing source of both irritation and inspiration for various Christian camps and a catalyst for much debate.

The phrase "perfect Christian" often conjures up images of humans that have achieved the status of some sterile, stainless steel, sanctified robots with a direct cable to heaven from which they receive their divine signals.

At first glance, we might assume that Jesus has asked us to be inhuman—holy angelic androids—but a closer look provides a much clearer picture. In the New Testament, the word "perfect" appears 42 times and is usually translated from the Greek "teleios" (tel'-i-os). Strong defines it as "complete in labor, growth, mental and moral character, etc., of full age." Here are a few other examples where "teleios" is used:

- "I in them, and thou in me, that they may be made perfect in one" (John 17:23).

- "Let us therefore, as many as be perfect, be thus minded" (Philippians 3:15).

- "If any man offend not in word, the same is a perfect man" (James 3:2).

The word "perfect" is found in the Old Testament about 57 times, and it is usually translated from the Hebrew word "tamiym" (taw-meem'), which Strong defines as "entire, integrity, truth, without blemish, complete, full, perfect, sincerely, sound, without spot, undefiled, upright, whole."

- "Noah was a just man, perfect in his generations" (Genesis 6:9).

- "I am the Almighty God; walk before me, and be thou perfect" (Genesis 17:1).

- "Thou shalt be perfect with the LORD thy God" (Deuteronomy 18:13).

THE TABOO TOPIC

The subject of Christian perfection is such a volatile theological issue among Christians that most preachers refuse to venture anywhere near it. If a minister is bold enough to admit that he believes God wants us to stop sinning, then he becomes an instant target for the question, "Have you stopped sinning?"

Well, here I go: I believe that God wants us to stop sinning.

"Pastor Doug, have you stopped sinning?"

No. But I'm also in good company. Paul also confessed he had not yet arrived. *"Not as though I had already attained, either were already perfect: but I follow after, if that I may apprehend that for which also I am apprehended of Christ Jesus. Brethren, I count not myself to have apprehended: but this one thing I do, forgetting those things which are behind, and reaching forth unto those things which are before; I press toward the mark for the prize of the high calling of God in Christ Jesus"* (Philippians 3:12–14).

Furthermore, we are not to interpret truth based on my, or anyone else's, personal experience. The idea that we are saved with our sins and not ultimately from our sins has grown out of a popular tendency to interpret the Bible based on a majority consensus.

I have heard hundreds of people say that they believe most politicians lie on a regular basis—almost as if it were part of their job description. So often, when it comes time to vote, we choose the most likeable liar.

In the same way, because there are so many counterfeit Christians, most people have come to believe that the concept of a perfect Christian is as remote as finding an honest politician. However, the Lord has made it clear that though consistent obedience is rare, it is possible.

"And the Lord said unto Satan, Hast thou considered my servant Job, that there is none like him in the earth, a perfect and an upright man, one that feareth God, and escheweth evil?" (Job 2:3). *"Because strait is the gate, and narrow is the way, which leadeth unto life, and few there be that find it"* (Matthew 7:14).

Since there is so much failure and imperfection in the world and the church, many have concluded that God is content for the saints to wear crooked halos until Jesus comes. But I believe that although we are not called to be robots, we are commanded to be perfectly surrendered.

I like the way Dr. A.J. Gordon says it: "We gravely fear that many Christians make the Apostle's word, 'If we say that we have no sin, we deceive ourselves,' the unconscious justification for a low standard of Christian living. It were almost better for one to overstate the possibilities of sanctification in his eager grasp after holiness, than to understate them in his complacent satisfaction with a traditional unholiness. ... If we regard the doctrine of sinless perfection as a heresy, we regard contentment with sinful imperfection as a greater heresy."

DOES GOD WANT PERFECTION?

Of course He does! How can a perfect, holy God be content with an imperfect standard? Or how can a perfect Creator, who originally made a perfect creation, be satisfied with an imperfect one? Here's the next question: Does God ever tolerate imperfection? Once again, of course! Otherwise He would destroy you and me on the spot. In fact, the whole world would be instantly destroyed if God did not at least temporarily tolerate imperfection. Although it is perfectly clear that Jesus did not come to condemn sinners, neither did He come to condone sin!

Remember the story in the Gospel of John about the woman who was caught in the act of adultery? According to the law, she was to be stoned. Many believe her to be Mary Magdalene, and this was her first encounter with Jesus.

As Mary stood trembling before Jesus awaiting her sentencing, Jesus wrote in the dust. One by one, her accusers left.

When Jesus stood up and saw no one but the woman, He said to her, "*Woman, where are those thine accusers? Hath no man condemned thee?*" (John 8:10).

I believe she read love and compassion in Jesus' face. She believed in His grace and she received it when He said, "*Neither do I condemn thee.*" But lest we misunderstand the deadly nature of sin, He plainly added, "*go, and sin no more*" (verse 11).

Is Jesus asking us to be sinless? Absolutely. Jesus can never ask anything less. Sin was the disease destroying Mary. What would you have Jesus say? "Go and sin a little less" or "Go and cut back on your life of sin"? Jesus did not come to save us with our sin but from our sin (Matthew 1:21)—that means from the penalty, the power and ultimately the presence of sin.

REAL REPENTANCE

Some say that when Jesus told Mary, *"Neither do I condemn thee; go, and sin no more,"* it proved that the law had been set aside. In fact, the opposite is true! *"Sin is the transgression of the law"* (1 John 3:4). Jesus was telling Mary, "I will take your penalty because I love you. Sin hurts you and sin hurts me. I will be a sacrifice in your place, go and sin (break the law) no more."

But in Scripture, real repentance consistently calls for sorrow for, and turning from, the sin as a condition for mercy. *"He that covereth his sins shall not prosper: but whoso confesseth and forsaketh them shall have mercy"* (Proverbs 28:13). *"If we confess our sins, he is faithful and just to forgive us our sins, and to cleanse us from all unrighteousness"* (1 John 1:9).

Sarah was a wonderful Christian woman who had a rare and deep relationship with the Lord. But her brother George was the proverbial black sheep of the family, and his selfish life was the antithesis of his sister's generous conduct. George had a severe alcohol problem. After years of abuse, his body began to rebel from the constant drinking, and his kidneys were failing fast. The doctors told Sarah that George would surely die soon without a kidney transplant, but it was doubtful that he would even qualify to be placed on the waiting list for a kidney because of his steady history of drinking. Sarah asked the doctors if she could give one of her kidneys to her ailing brother. The doctors responded, "If your blood types match, yes. But this is an expensive operation, and we question the wisdom of putting your health at risk for a person with such self-destructive habits."

It turned out that their blood types did match, but George had no insurance, so Sarah quickly mortgaged her home and promised she would pay the rest. With some persistent urging, she finally persuaded the hospital to perform the surgery.

The transplant procedure went fine, for George that is, but there were some tragic complications for Sarah.

She had a severe allergic reaction to the anesthetic and found herself paralyzed after the surgery from the waist down. Sarah was able to bravely bear the tragic news when she was told that George was doing remarkably well. She said, "If I am able to buy my brother a few more years of life to find the Savior then it was still worth it, even if I can never walk again."

Now here is the reason for the story. How do you think Sarah felt when her brother never stopped by her bed to thank her for her costly sacrifice? And how do you think Sarah felt when she learned that the first thing her brother did after leaving the hospital was to go to the bar and celebrate?

Most of the world eagerly takes the blessings of God and then selfishly squanders them like the prodigal son. But how do you think Jesus feels when a professed Christian goes from His presence after receiving mercy and life and returns to the very thing that cost Him such suffering to save us? When we see and understand something of how much our sins have cost Him, we will no longer want to embrace the monster that ravaged our Lord.

Jesus did not come and die on the cross to purchase us a license for us to sin. He came to save us from sin. That love is the power that enables us to turn from sin. *"Or despisest thou the riches of His goodness and forbearance and longsuffering; not knowing that the goodness of God leadeth thee to repentance?"* (Romans 2:4).

SEVENTY TIMES SEVEN

B ecause we might repeat the same mistakes and fall into the same sin more than once does not mean that God has forsaken us. Evidently, Mary Magdalene had the same struggle.

"And certain women, which had been healed of evil spirits and infirmities, Mary called Magdalene, out of whom went seven devils" (Luke 8:2). This does not mean that Jesus cast out seven demons at one time, but rather seven times she slipped back into the old patterns of sin and He forgave her. *"For a just man falleth seven times, and riseth up again"* (Proverbs 24:16).

Do not become discouraged if, like Mary, you find yourself repenting of the same mistakes several times. Jesus said, *"Take heed to yourselves: If thy brother trespass against thee, rebuke him; and if he repent, forgive him. And if he trespass against thee seven times in a day, and seven times in a day turn again to thee, saying, I repent; thou shalt forgive him"* (Luke 17:3, 4).

"Then Peter came to him and said, Lord, how oft shall my brother sin against me, and I forgive him? till seven times? Jesus saith unto him, I say not unto thee, Until seven times: but, Until seventy times seven" (Matthew 18:21, 22). If God is asking us to forgive each other seven

times in one day or seventy times seven, will He do less for us? Of course, God will forgive us every time that we sincerely repent.

But there is a danger that we can come to the place where we presume on His grace and through abusing His forgiveness, harden our own hearts. *"For if we sin wilfully after that we have received the knowledge of the truth, there remaineth no more sacrifice for sins"* (Hebrews 10:26).

The first verses of Romans 6 adds, *"What shall we say then? Shall we continue in sin, that grace may abound? God forbid. How shall we, that are dead to sin, live any longer therein?"*

There is effort involved in denying self and living the Christian life. The Bible says we war, wrestle, run, fight and strive. But the fight is a good fight of faith. We must strive to trust God's plan and will for us rather than our own. We must fight to stay close to Jesus. Mary was safe from sin when she was with Jesus. *"Whosoever abideth in him sinneth not"* (1 John 3:6).

CHRISTIANS FOLLOW CHRIST

The bottom line is that Jesus came to this planet for three primary reasons. First, to show us the Father (John 14:9, 10). Second, to die as our substitute for our sins (1 Corinthians 15:3; 1 John 4:10). Third, to give us an example of how to be victorious. Notice the ways we are invited to mirror Jesus:

- *"As my Father hath sent me, even so send I you"* (John 20:21).

- *"For even hereunto were ye called, because Christ also suffered for us, leaving us an example, that ye should follow his steps"* (1 Peter 2:21).

- *"For I have given you an example, that ye should do as I have done to you"* (John 13:15).

- *"Forbearing one another, and forgiving one another, if any man have a quarrel against any: even as Christ forgave you, so also do ye"* (Colossians 3:13).

- *"A new commandment I give unto you, That ye love one another; as I have loved you, that you also love one another"* (John 13:34).

We are sent into the world as Jesus was sent, commanded to walk as He walked, do as He did, forgive as He forgave, and love as He loved! In light of these plain principles, why would a professed Christian resist the truth that we are called to be holy (perfect) as He is holy?

Many might claim that I'm nothing more than a perfectionist. Once again, I certainly do not claim to be perfect, but every Christian is a follower of a perfect Savior. Jesus left us a perfect example. And just as soon as we say that God cannot keep us from sinning, we venture onto deadly ground. In essence, we are saying, "Satan is powerful enough to tempt me to sin, but Jesus is not powerful enough to keep me from sin." Yet my Bible tells me, *"Greater is he that is in you, than he that is in the world"* (1 John 4:4).

He who attempts to justify his sin, negates his justification. The central issue of Jesus' mission was to save us from sin's penalty and power. *"He who committeth sin is of the devil; for the devil sinneth from the beginning. For this purpose the Son of God was manifested, that he might destroy the works of the devil"* (1 John 3:8).

The undisputed work of the devil is to tempt us to sin, and Jesus came to shatter those shackles that bind us and set the captives free (Isaiah 61:1).

CONSISTENT OBEDIENCE

If you really think about it, everybody obeys God some of the time—at least while they're sleeping. But the Lord is looking for a people who will obey Him consistently. That's why the Lord told Moses, *"Oh that there were such an heart in them, that they would fear me, and keep all my commandments always, that it might be well with them, and with their children for ever!"* (Deuteronomy 5:29). Notice that the Lord asks us to keep all of His commandments always—not to make us miserable, but for our and our children's ultimate happiness!

King Darius said to Daniel, *"Thy God whom thou servest continually, he will deliver thee"* (Daniel 6:16). Keep in mind that the ones who do obey God consistently are often the last ones to be aware of it. (In fact, you should avoid anyone who parades his or her so-called perfection.)

In addition, when Daniel had a vision of God, he said, *"My comeliness was turned in me into corruption"* (Daniel 10:8). This is because the closer we come to the light of God, the more aware we become of our imperfections.

One of my favorite Christian writers put it best: "One ray of the glory of God, one gleam of the purity of Christ, penetrating the soul, makes every spot of defilement painfully distinct, and lays bare the deformity and defects of the human character. ... He loathes himself as he views the pure, spotless character of Christ."

PROMISES OF POWER TO OBEY

The Bible is overrunning with *"exceeding great and precious promises: that by these ye might be partakers of the divine nature, having escaped the corruption that is in the world through lust"* (2 Peter 1:4).

Here are just a few:

- *"Mark the perfect man, and behold the upright: for the end of that man is peace"* (Psalm 37:37).

- *"Nay, in all these things we are more than conquerors through him that loved us"* (Romans 8:37).

- *"Now thanks be unto God, who always causeth us to triumph in Christ, and maketh manifest the saviour of his knowledge by us in every place"* (2 Corinthians 2:14).

- *"Wherefore he is able also to save them to the uttermost that come unto God by him"* (Hebrews 7:25).

- *"Now unto him that is able to keep you from falling, and to present you faultless before the presence of his glory with exceeding joy"* (Jude 1:24).

- *"For the grace of God that bringeth salvation hath appeared to all men, Teaching us that, denying ungodliness and worldly lusts, we should live soberly, righteously, and godly, in the present world"* (Titus 2:11, 12).

Those who refuse to believe that we can live victorious lives are accusing God of a gross and cruel injustice: Asking us to do the impossible, then punishing us for not doing it. That would be something like a father telling his three-foot toddler to touch the ceiling that rises up seven feet—and while the little one is straining on his tiptoes, the father hits the child to the ground and yells, "I told you to touch the ceiling and you disobeyed me!" An ugly picture indeed.

But suppose instead that I ask my toddler to touch the ceiling and, as he is straining and stretching to do the impossible, I gently reach down and lift him up to his goal. This is how the Bible pictures God. Within every command of God there is inherent the power to obey.

For example, God says, *"Ye shall be holy: for I the LORD your God am holy"* (Leviticus 19:2).

Also, *"As he which hath called you is holy, so be ye holy in all manner of conversation"* (1 Peter 1:15). Notice the word "be." When the Lord created the world He said, *"Let there **be** Light, and there was light"* (Genesis 1:3, emphasis added).

When Jesus cleansed the leper, He said, *"Be thou clean."* And he became clean! Likewise, when Jesus said, *"Be ye therefore perfect"* (Matthew 5:48), the enabling power itself is in the divine word "be." I know that when God asks us to live a holy life, it seems at times unattainable, but remember, when God asks us to cross an ocean without a boat, He will either part the sea or enable us to walk on water.

Jesus said, *"Without me ye can do nothing"* (John 15:5). And Paul added, *"I can do all things through Christ which strengtheneth me"* (Philippians 4:13).

PERFECT LOVE

So what is the essence of Christian perfection? If we look at the context of Matthew 5, Jesus is speaking of loving our enemies. When we reach verse 48 and Jesus says, *"Be ye therefore perfect, even as your Father which is in heaven is perfect,"* it becomes clear that He is talking about perfect love. Further proof for this concept is seen in Luke 6:36, where Jesus words it differently: *"Be ye therefore merciful, as your Father is also merciful."*

So what is Christian perfection? Perfect love and perfect mercy. Perfect love is demonstrated in a willingness to obey. *"If ye love me, keep my commandments"* (John 14:15). For example, Shadrach, Meshach and Abed-nego loved God more than their own lives and were willing to go to the fiery furnace rather than dishonor Him. And Daniel was willing to go to the lions' den rather than be ashamed of his God. Though this love is rare, it is real and attainable for all who believe!

FAITH IN THE VICTORY

Sin is more than a single offense; sin is a lifestyle. Before Jesus saves us, we are slaves to sin. After Jesus saves us, we may still slip, but *"Sin shall not have dominion over you"* (Romans 6:14). For the Christian, where sin once sat enthroned and unchallenged, Jesus now sits as Lord and King on the throne of our hearts.

"Let not sin therefore reign in your mortal body, that ye should obey it in the lusts thereof" (Romans 6:12).

This does not mean that genuine Christians will not make mistakes. There are too many examples in the Bible where they do. This is why John said, *"My little children, these things I write unto you, that ye sin not. And if any man sin, we have an advocate with the Father, Jesus Christ the righteous"* (1 John 2:1). However, the mistakes should be the exception, not the rule.

This concept is clearly described in a famous book called *Steps to Christ*. "The character is revealed, not by occasional good deeds and occasional misdeeds, but by the tendency of the habitual words and acts" (57).

During World War II, General Jonathan Wainwright was captured by the Japanese and held prisoner in a Manchurian concentration camp. Cruelly treated, he outwardly appeared a broken, crushed, hopeless, and starving man. Finally the Japanese surrendered and the war ended. A U.S. Army colonel came to the prison camp and announced to the general that Japan had been defeated and that he was free and in command.

After Wainwright heard the news, he returned to his quarters where he was confronted by some Japanese guards who began to mistreat him as they had done in the past. However, Wainwright, with the news of victory still fresh in his mind, declared with authority, "Now I am in command here! These are my orders." From that moment on, General Wainwright was in control.

General Wainwright had received word from a higher power, and he acted in faith on that word and it became real. He would no longer acknowledge the authority of his tormentors. When we accept the truth that Jesus now reigns and has "all authority" and is with us always, we too can be free indeed! *"My eyes shall be upon the faithful of the land, that they may dwell with me: he that walketh in a perfect way, he shall serve me"* (Psalm 101:6).

"For whatsoever is born of God overcometh the world: and this is the victory that overcometh the world, even our faith" (1 John 5:4).

THE PERIL OF SMOOTH THINGS
CHAPTER EIGHT

"**N**ow go, write it before them in a table, and note it in a book, that it may be for the time to come for ever and ever: That this is a rebellious people, lying children, children that will not bear the law of the LORD: Which say to the seers, See not; and to the prophets, Prophesy not unto us right things, speak unto us smooth things, prophesy deceits" (Isaiah 30: 8–10).

A Protestant missionary who worked among the natives in the South Pacific for several years decided to return to the United States for a nine-month furlough. During this time, he planned to visit several churches and raise funds for their island mission. Before leaving the South Pacific, this missionary persuaded a local chief, who had converted to Christianity, to join him on his trip. This tall chief had an imposing presence with a dark, muscular body that was offset by his broad, pearly white smile. The missionary knew that a living trophy of their mission efforts would greatly impress the church members in North America to give more generously.

Excited about an opportunity to see the famous U.S.A., the robust king agreed to go with his pastor friend to the mainland. When they arrived, the missionary took the chief from church to church. The missionary would show slides of their mission station, then parade the chief in his colorful native costume and tell of his conversion from paganism.

However, as they journeyed between churches, the missionary decided to dress his island friend in typical western garments to avoid the gawking of onlookers. It was hard to find a pair of shoes wide enough for the burly native's rough feet, but they finally succeeded. To make their travel easier, the chief also began to eat American food. But after the nine-month whirlwind tour during which they visited scores of churches across the United States, the western lifestyle began to take its toll on the Polynesian king. His feet softened from wearing shoes, and he lost the definition and tone in his muscles due to a lack of exercise. Worse still, because the chief was unaccustomed to such sweet, highly processed and refined foods, he began to lose his teeth and suffer frequent stomach ailments.

By the time they returned to the chief's island home, he had drooping shoulders and soft feet. Where once there was muscle, there was now flab. He had so many missing teeth and such pale skin that many of his own villagers could barely recognize him. He was nearly ruined by "soft living."

BABY FOOD

In the same way that soft food and soft living make us physically weak, a diet of overly refined and fiber-less spiritual pabulum produces a church full of weak, infantile invalids. Physicians are constantly reminding us that to be healthy, we must have sufficient roughage in our diets. This also applies to our spiritual diet. Unfortunately, many Christians have been gumming baby mush for so long that they are offended by real food.

"For though by this time you ought to be teachers, you need someone to teach you again the first principles of the oracles of God; and you have come to need milk and not solid food. For everyone who partakes only of milk is unskilled in the word of righteousness, for he is a babe. But solid food belongs to those who are of full age, that is, those who by reason of use have their senses exercised to discern both good and evil" (Hebrews 5:12–14, NKJV).

TASTY TERMINOLOGY

In North America especially, our brains and bodies are slowly being destroyed by convenience stores, elevators, auto dial and remote control. This love for soft, smooth living has also begun to infect the church. In this age of fast food, everyone wants a sermonette. (A friend of mine once said, "Sermonettes are for Christianettes.") And so, to secure popularity among their comfort-loving members, many pastors are falling into the same pattern as those politicians who travel from one district to another telling everybody what they think will please them. What follows is a list of some of the smooth and popular (yet poisonous) doctrines of demons that pastors are telling their flocks:

● Once you're saved, you can't be lost.

● It's not necessary to keep the literal Sabbath commandment as long as you are "resting in Jesus."

● The second coming of Jesus might be centuries in the future, so don't be concerned.

● As long as you pray over your food, you can eat or drink anything without suffering the normal consequences.

● Abortion is not really killing an unborn baby; it's a "pregnancy termination."

● Practicing homosexuality is not really a sin; it's simply an alternative lifestyle.

● God is going to rapture His church before the tribulation, so we won't have to experience any fiery trials.

● Jesus came to save us with (or in) our sins rather than from them.

In essence, the church is striving so hard to be politically correct and sensitive to the world that it has become indifferent before God!

CALLING SIN BY ITS RIGHT NAME

The devil wants to soothe our consciences to sleep, lest we should awake to our peril and turn from our sins. He is afraid that we will discover how lethal sin really is and then start looking for a Savior! Paul puts it this way: *"That sin by the commandment might become exceeding sinful"* (Romans 7:13).

My grandfather smoked those pungent Lucky Strike cigarettes for years. He made a few feeble attempts to quit smoking, but because his health was fair, he was not too alarmed and therefore not very motivated. Then one day he was admitted into the hospital for a simple procedure and was appalled when he saw the man in the bed next to him smoking Lucky Strike cigarettes through a hole in his throat. The man's voice box had been removed due to a smoking-related cancer. That was all the motivation my grandfather needed. As soon as he understood how exceedingly dangerous smoking really is, he threw away his cigarettes and has never smoked since. He was as healthy as anyone after he quit.

If a doctor is so afraid to upset you that he says you have a touch of poison ivy when really you have leprosy, then he is not your friend. Likewise, as Christians, we should honestly diagnose sin so that it can receive the appropriate treatment. Proverbs 27:6 says, *"Faithful are the wounds of a friend; but the kisses of an enemy are deceitful."* Ministers and church members alike have a responsibility to faithfully and lovingly warn the world around them that there is a heaven to win and a hell to shun. People need to understand that persisting to live a life of sin will end in eternal and irrevocable loss.

"So thou, O son of man, I have set thee a watchman unto the house of Israel; therefore thou shalt hear the word at my mouth, and warn them from me. When I say unto the wicked, O wicked man, thou shalt surely die; if thou dost not speak to warn the wicked from his way, that wicked man shall die in his iniquity; but his blood will I require at thine hand. Nevertheless, if thou warn the wicked of his way to turn from it; if he do not turn from his way, he shall die in his iniquity; but thou hast delivered thy soul" (Ezekiel 33:7–9).

As we near the end of the world and see the imminence of Jesus' second coming, now is not the time to proclaim smooth things. Every gospel presentation should be saturated with a sense of power and urgency. Isaiah 58:1 admonishes, *"Cry aloud, spare not, lift up thy voice like a trumpet, and shew my people their transgression, and the house of Jacob their sins."*

Yet Jesus has told us that one of the signs of the end is that the church will be softly singing Satan's lying lullaby, "Rest in peace, in your sins." In 1 Thessalonians 5:3, God says, *"When they shall say, Peace and safety; then sudden destruction cometh upon them, as travail* [labor pains] *upon a woman with child; and they shall not escape."* I used to believe that this Scripture was speaking only of the world, but now I know that Paul was also warning us of conditions within the church!

THE TRUTH CAN HURT

I have attended too many funerals where I had to listen to the pastor preach the deceased person right into heaven even though the individual had made no profession of knowing or loving God. Later, when I ask the minister about this, his response was usually something like this: "Well, you know, the family is grieving and I thought it would make them feel better." Such men think they are doing people a favor by preaching smooth things, but as a result of their carelessness, scores of others leave the funeral thinking that everyone is going to be saved regardless of how they lived or whether they made a profession of faith.

On many occasions, Jesus had to say some rough things—not to be abrasive, but for the purpose of saving souls. And on more than one occasion, droves of followers turned away from Jesus because of His rough statements (John 6:60, 66).

I cannot improve on the following statement from the classic book *Steps to Christ*: "Jesus did not suppress one word of truth, but He uttered it always in love. He exercised the greatest tact and thoughtful, kind attention in His intercourse with the people. He was never rude, never needlessly spoke a severe word, never gave needless pain to a sensitive soul. He did not censure human weakness. He spoke the truth, but always in love. He denounced hypocrisy, unbelief, and iniquity; but tears were in His voice as He uttered His scathing rebukes" (p. 12).

The hard sayings of Jesus were never designed to wound or offend, but rather to save us and help us grow the fruits of the Spirit. Jesus said, *"Every branch in me that beareth not fruit he taketh away: and every branch that beareth fruit, he purgeth it, that it may bring forth more fruit"* (John 15:2).

And in Hebrews 12:11, Paul wrote, *"Now no chastening for the present seemeth to be joyous, but grievous: nevertheless afterward it yieldeth the peaceable fruit of righteousness unto them which are exercised thereby."*

FALSE PROPHETS

Jesus has warned us that in the last days, there will be many false prophets preaching smooth things (Matthew 24:11). That's why we must know how to distinguish the true from the counterfeit. To take the high, straight, and rough road of biting honesty when everyone else is sliding down the smooth road buttered with popular platitudes requires a rare and unusual breed of courage. In the first book of Kings, we find a story that dramatically illustrates how most people in this world are hungering to hear smooth things, yet God still has His faithful ones who want to hear and tell the truth at any cost.

Ahab, the wicked king of Israel, wanted to recapture the town of Ramoth-gilead from the Syrians, but he needed help to take on the superior army of Syria. So Ahab asked King Jehoshaphat of Judah to join him in a campaign against their common enemy. Jehoshaphat said that he was willing to join forces with Ahab but that they should first seek God's council.

Ahab had forsaken the Lord years earlier to worship the pagan god Baal, so he called in 400 hired prophets to come before the two monarchs and prophesy. From their magnificent thrones, the two kings watched as the false prophets, with a loud and dramatic display, said, "Go and fight the Syrians, and you will be victorious!" Judging by outward appearance, it was a very impressive pep rally. But Jehoshaphat remained skeptical and again requested to hear from a prophet of the Lord. With great reluctance, Ahab conceded that there was one prophet of Jehovah still living whose name was Micaiah. But he added, *"I hate him; for he doth not prophesy good concerning me, but evil"* (1 Kings 22:8).

Nevertheless, at Jehoshaphat's urging, Ahab sent a servant to fetch Micaiah, the prophet of God. When the king's messenger found Micaiah, he told him, *"Behold now, the words of the [false] prophets declare good unto the king with one mouth: let thy word, I pray thee, be like the word of one of them, and speak that which is good"* (1 Kings 22:13). Ahab's servant was advising God's prophet to preach smooth things! Micaiah replied, *"As the LORD liveth, what the LORD saith unto me, that will I speak"* (1 Kings 22:14). Now there's a novel thought! Tell the truth, regardless of the consequences. The brave prophet appeared before the monarchs and clearly told Ahab that if he went to fight the Syrians, he would surely die in the battle. Now Ahab was faced with a tough decision. Should he believe 400 prophets who preach smooth things, or one lone prophet of the Lord who delivers a rough message?

Stubborn Ahab persuaded Jehoshaphat to disregard the warnings of Micaiah and join him in the war. After all, how could one negative prophet be right and 400 optimistic prophets be wrong? Ahab thought he could outsmart the Lord by dressing in full armor and staying away from the frontlines of battle. But he learned too late that you can never escape the Word of God. In the midst of the conflict, a stray arrow flying through the air struck Ahab in the joints of his armor, and he bled to death in his chariot. Ahab was killed by embracing the fatal flatteries of false prophets.

Jesus warned, *"Woe unto you, when all men shall speak well of you! for so did their fathers to the false prophets"* (Luke 6:26). And the prophet Jeremiah put it this way, *"Believe them not, though they speak fair words unto thee"* (Jeremiah 12:6).

An Upward Challenge

The apostle Paul tells us that in the last days, one of the characteristics of the church is that members will look for ministers to tell them what pleases the carnal nature—for smooth, easy religion without a cross. He says in 2 Timothy 4:2–4: *"Preach the word; Be instant in season, out of season; reprove, rebuke, exhort with all longsuffering and doctrine. For the time will come when they will not endure sound doctrine; but after their own lusts shall they heap to themselves teachers, having itching ears; And they shall turn away their ears from the truth, and shall be turned unto fables."* People want a form of religion, but not the power to overcome their sins (2 Timothy 3:5).

In an effort to "give the people what they want," many churches provide bazaars, bingo and soothing social programs but do not preach salvation from sin. Their sermons are like a saw with no teeth. The sharp sword of God's Word is being replaced with a rubber-coated baby spoon! It's no wonder that people leave such worship services feeling like they have been feasting on molasses. It was sweet to eat, but afterward everyone walks away sticky and nauseated.

Abraham Lincoln was riding home from church in his carriage one Sunday when his secretary asked how he liked the sermon. "Not very much," said the president. His response surprised the secretary because the preacher was popular and most people considered him a very gifted speaker. When asked what the problem was, Lincoln replied, "He did not ask me to do anything great."

The true Word of God will always challenge us to press onward and upward to great things.

READ THE LABEL

As I am aging and becoming more concerned with maintaining good health, I have found myself reading the ingredients on food labels more carefully. "Reading the label" is also a good practice for spiritual shopping. Proverbs 23:1–3 says, "*When thou sittest to eat with a ruler, consider diligently what is before thee: And put a knife to thy throat, if thou be a man given to appetite. Be not desirous of his* [Satan's sweet] *dainties: for they are deceitful meat.*"

So what can we do to resist the temptation of gobbling up Satan's sweet but deceptive delicacies?

1. Measure all teachings by the Word of God. "*To the law and to the testimony: if they speak not according to this word, it is because there is no light in them*" (Isaiah 8:20).

2. Be willing to do God's will whatever the consequences! "*If any man will do his will, he shall know of the doctrine, whether it be of God*" (John 7:17).

3. Never accept a teaching just because it is popular. "*Thou shalt not follow a multitude to do evil*" (Exodus 23:2).

4. Place yourself under a well-balanced diet of spiritual teaching, and feed your own soul with God's Word and other inspired reading. "*Study to shew thyself approved unto God, a workman that needeth not to be ashamed, rightly dividing the word of truth*" (2 Timothy 2:15).

A FAITHFUL FOCUS

Several years ago, a man living in China bought a microscope. At first, he was thrilled with his new acquisition and marveled as he looked at the wonders of flowers and feathers magnified hundreds of times. But one day he made the mistake of looking at his rice under the microscope and saw that it was crawling with tiny creatures. Rice was his favorite food. Very disturbed, the man smashed his microscope with a rock. It had revealed that his rice had bugs, and he didn't want to give up his beloved staple.

We are all faced with a similar challenge. We can either place ourselves under the scrutiny of God's Word and allow Him to boil away the bugs, or else we can turn the microscope of His law out of focus to blur our character defects. Those who choose the truth of God over the fancy fables of false prophets will follow the advice found in Scripture: *"Examine yourselves, whether ye be in the faith; prove your own selves"* (2 Corinthians 13:5).

May our sincere prayer be like that of David, who said, *"Search me, O God, and know my heart: try me, and know my thoughts: And see if there be any wicked way in me, and lead me in the way everlasting"* (Psalm 139:23, 24).

POWER IN PURITY
CHAPTER NINE

An Amazing Fact: A remarkable little spider in Asia makes its home under water. The "water spider" spins a petite web in the shape of a bell and attaches it to stems of waterweeds and plants just below the pond surface. All spiders breathe air, so this one takes its air along like a skin diver. On the surface, it traps tiny bubbles in the hairs of its body, then hurries home and releases them under its web. The spider makes many trips to bring air bubbles back home. The waterproof web then becomes inflated with trapped air and makes a perfect diving bell where the little monster lives, eats and lays eggs. If the air is used up, the spider surfaces to breathe and collects more fresh bubbles. Living below, and yet breathing the air from above, this little spider is constantly surrounded by water—yet remains perfectly dry!

The water spider knows a vital secret that represents the essence of what every Christian must learn. It lives in the water, a foreign realm, and yet remains separate from it, maintained by contact from above. In a sense, this illustrates how Christians can sojourn in this wicked world without being polluted by it.

The Word of God is very clear—purity of heart is a crucial prerequisite for salvation and entrance to heaven:

- *"Follow peace with all men, and holiness, without which no man shall see the Lord"* (Hebrews 12:14).

- *"Blessed are the pure in heart: for they shall see God"* (Matthew 5:8).

- *"And there shall in no wise enter into it any thing that defileth, neither whatsoever worketh abomination, or maketh a lie: but they which are written in the Lamb's book of life"* (Revelation 21:27).

One of the most complex challenges for Christians is learning how to live in this impure world without allowing the world to live in us. How are we to work for and reach the lost without living like the lost? Jesus came, in part, to demonstrate how to balance loving and redeeming the publicans and prostitutes without walking in their ways. Like the water spider, the key is found in learning how to breathe the atmosphere of heaven while existing in this evil empire below. Jesus outlined this challenge when praying to the Father.

"I have given them thy word; and the world hath hated them, because they are not of the world, even as I am not of the world. I pray not that thou shouldest take them out of the world, but that thou shouldest keep them from the evil" (John 17:14, 15).

Ambassadors and Embassies

The most crucial secret for enjoying purity of heart is to follow Jesus' example of maintaining constant communication with the Father. *"And in the morning, rising up a great while before day, he went out, and departed into a solitary place, and there prayed"* (Mark 1:35).

The American embassies located throughout the world all have a dedicated "hotline" phone so they can stay in continual communication with their mother government. They give reports and receive regular instructions from their superiors regarding how to represent the United States in these foreign fields. They also serve as a haven, giving assistance to American citizens or those who might want to seek asylum and become citizens.

Our churches are something like embassies in a strange land, and each Christian is an ambassador for the kingdom of heaven. Only through regular prayer, Bible study and church attendance can we thrive in this world as ambassadors of another kingdom without adopting the customs of the enemy. This is our only hope to maintain our independence from the devil's government and preserve the purity of heart that is a trademark of the redeemed.

"These all died in faith... and confessed that they were strangers and pilgrims on the earth" (Hebrews 11:13).

STARTING INSIDE

A common mistake in approaching the concept of purity is to think that if we can convince others that we are pure, God will give us credit for their votes of confidence. This was the flawed philosophy of the Pharisees who did their praying, fasting, and giving to be seen of men (Matthew 6). Paul comments, *"But they measuring themselves by themselves, and comparing themselves among themselves, are not wise"* (2 Corinthians 10:12).

Jesus made it plain that all acts of outward holiness that do not spring from the new heart are, in reality, hypocrisy. God sees the attitude as well as the action. Authentic purity must first be born in the heart before the fruit of holiness can be seen in the life. This principle of inward purity is found all through the Scriptures:

- *"Cleanse first that which is within the cup and platter, that the outside of them may be clean also"* (Matthew 23:26).

- *"Cleanse your hands, ye sinners; and purify your hearts, ye double minded"* (James 4:8).

- *"Seeing ye have purified your souls in obeying the truth through the Spirit unto unfeigned love of the brethren, see that ye love one another with a pure heart fervently"* (1 Peter 1:22).

SALVATION AND PURIFICATION

It's clear enough that we need new and pure hearts, but where do we begin? The science of salvation is really about a process of purification. It begins with the free gift of a pure life record. When we confess our sins and accept the sacrifice and blood of Jesus to cover our transgressions, we are justified by virtue of the pure merits of Jesus' life. God the Father gives us credit for the spotless life of His Son and looks upon us with approval as if we never had sinned.

- *"He that covereth his sins shall not prosper: but whoso confesseth and forsaketh them shall have mercy"* (Proverbs 28:13).

- *"If we confess our sins, he is faithful and just to forgive us our sins, and to cleanse us from all unrighteousness"* (1 John 1:9).

As we accept this incredible gift by faith, a new heart and a desire to preserve this new experience and relationship is born within us. But even this act of total surrender is possible only through God's power.

As my favorite Christian author puts it: "No outward observances can take the place of simple faith and entire renunciation of self. But no man can empty himself of self. We can only consent for Christ to accomplish the work. Then the language of the soul will be, Lord, take my heart; for I cannot give it. It is Thy property. Keep it pure, for I cannot keep it for Thee. Save me in spite of myself, my weak, unchristlike self. Mold me, fashion me, raise me into a pure and holy atmosphere, where the rich current of Thy love can flow through my soul" (*Christ's Object Lessons*, 159).

It is not necessary that we understand all the dynamics of how this metamorphosis operates to enjoy its benefits. Evangelist Billy Sunday once said, "I cannot explain how blood can wash away sin, but I also do not know how a black cow can eat green grass and make white milk and yellow butter, but I still enjoy milk and butter."

A NEW POINT OF REFERENCE

We've learned that the starting point is simply to receive Jesus into our hearts, *"That Christ may dwell in your hearts by faith"* (Ephesians 3:17). He stands knocking at the door of our hearts, but we must choose to let Him in (Revelation 3:20).

As we allow Him to abide there by faith, He has a purifying influence—*"Purifying their hearts by faith"* (Acts 15:9).

I once read an interesting story about a rather rough, uncultured bachelor. This man fell in love with a beautiful vase he saw in a shop window each day as he went to and from work. Eventually the man bought this exquisite vase and put it on the mantelpiece by the window in his room. There, its beauty stood out in stark contrast with the messy apartment, and it became a bold judgment on its surroundings. He had to clean up the room to make it worthy of the vase. The curtains looked drab and faded beside it. The old chair with the stuffing peeking out no longer fit in. The peeling wallpaper and paint needed renewing. Gradually, one project at a time, he had the whole room renovated until the beauty of this one object transformed all.

This story illustrates the same transforming influence that the presence of Jesus has when He is received into an impure heart. I cannot improve on the explanation of this process found in the book *Steps to Christ*:

"One ray of the glory of God, one gleam of the purity of Christ, penetrating the soul, makes every spot of defilement painfully distinct, and lays bare the deformity and defects of the human character. It makes apparent the unhallowed desires, the infidelity of the heart, the impurity of the lips. The sinner's acts of disloyalty in making void the law of God, are exposed to his sight, and his spirit is stricken and afflicted under the searching influence of the Spirit of God. He loathes himself as he views the pure, spotless character of Christ" (29).

This was the experience of Isaiah, Daniel, and John when they stood in the pure, blazing presence of the Almighty. They were overwhelmed with a sense of their own defilement and then longed for holiness. You too can experience how the *"goodness of God leadeth thee to repentance"* (Romans 2:4).

THERE IS POWER IN PURITY

Sir Galahad, a knight of King Arthur's Roundtable, was called the "Maiden Knight" because of his pure life. (Not to be confused with Sir Lancelot who had an affair with King Arthur's wife, Guinevere.) English poet Alfred Tennyson reports Sir Galahad as saying, "My strength is as the strength of ten, because my heart is pure."

We do not become strong for God by virtue of our own righteousness, but many professed Christians are handicapped in their service—a sense of their unforsaken sins cripples their confidence and saps the vitality from their faith.

Remember, it was after the disciples had spent 10 days in the upper room humbling themselves and putting aside their differences that God poured on them the power of the Spirit.

"The children of Israel could not stand before their enemies" when the secret sin of Achan was buried in the camp (Joshua 7:12). Gideon had to destroy the idol in his home before God could give him victory against the enemy (Judges 6:25). And, of course, Samson lost his strength by compromising his convictions with the temptress Delilah (Judges 16:19).

In contrast, when we know that our lives are in harmony with the will of God, we will enjoy a holy boldness and enter every battle like David, allied with omnipotence. There is power in purity!

"But they that wait upon the LORD shall renew their strength; they shall mount up with wings as eagles; they shall run, and not be weary; and they shall walk, and not faint" (Isaiah 40:31).

THE WORD IS OUR GAUGE

A visitor in the studio of a great painter found on an easel some very fine, brilliant gems. When asked why he kept them there, the painter replied: "I need them there to tune up my eyes. When I am working in so many different pigments, imperceptibly the sense of color distinction becomes weakened. By having the color of these pure unchanging gems before me to refresh my eyes, the sense of true color is constantly renewed just as the musician's tuning-fork helps him maintain the perfect pitch."

With the nebulous standards of the world ever evolving and drifting downward, most people have convinced themselves that their lives are good enough. But the values of the world will not be the basis of the great judgment. *"All the ways of a man are clean in his own eyes; but the LORD weigheth the spirits"* (Proverbs 16:2).

If we hope to combat having the pallet of our conscience numb to truth and our perception of holiness stretched out of tune, we must have our values calibrated each day by the pure, unchanging Word of God.

- *"The words of the LORD are pure words: as silver tried in a furnace of earth, purified seven times"* (Psalm 12:6).

- *"The commandment of the LORD is pure, enlightening the eyes"* (Psalm 19:8).

- *"Thy word is very pure: therefore thy servant loveth it"* (Psalm 119:140).

- *"Every word of God is pure"* (Proverbs 30:5).

When the pure Word is proclaimed, hearers discover that their lives are out of tune, and they will begin to long for the forgiveness Jesus offers. This was the experience of those who listened to Peter preaching the Word at Pentecost. Shaken to the core from their complacency, the Spirit awakened within them a yearning for pardon and purity.

"Now when they heard this, they were pricked in their heart, and said unto Peter and to the rest of the apostles, Men and brethren, what shall we do?" (Acts 2:37).

PURE FOOD?

N ow I'm going to take what only seems like a slight detour from the typical principles of purity—but it is just as important. Not only is it imperative that we *"desire the sincere milk of the word"* to grow in sanctification (1 Peter 2:2), but I believe this study would be incomplete without remembering that eating and drinking forbidden and impure physical food also weakens us spiritually.

The book of Daniel begins with four young men resolving that they would not defile themselves with the corrupt food offered them by the Babylonians. God rewarded their self-control with clear minds, long lives and pure hearts. There is power in purity. Many who eat rich diets loaded with fat and sweets wonder why they have no moral strength and little inclination to resist the temptations of the enemy. Their blood is so congested with bad nutrition that their brains are clouded and numb, and their ability to discern between good and evil is hindered.

I know that even as some are reading this they are thinking: *"Didn't Jesus say that it's not what goes into a man's mouth that defiles him, but what comes out?"* (Mark 7:18). True, but what enters the mouth can have a direct influence on what comes out. This is why drunks curse and shout! We cannot ignore the truth that the body and spirit are joined.

Likewise, a pure diet and healthy lifestyle will greatly enhance our ability to live holy lives.

WE ARE CHANGED BY BEHOLDING

A godly pastor was approached by a physician in his congregation who was concerned about the pastor's hectic schedule. Handing the minister some theater tickets, he said, "You work too hard. You need some recreation. Go to this movie and have a good time."

The pastor looked at the tickets knowing he could not conscientiously attend. He said kindly, "Thank you, but I can't take them. I can't go."

"Why not?" the physician asked.

"Doctor, it's this way: As a surgeon, when you operate, you scrub your hands meticulously until you are especially clean. You wouldn't dare operate with dirty hands. I'm a servant of Christ. I deal with precious human souls. I wouldn't dare to do my service with a dirty life." We must guard what we put into our minds as well as what we put into our bodies.

Probably the most lethal influences eroding the purity of the modern Christian are the TV and VCR. Many professed Christians who would never be found guilty of engaging in the actual deeds of murder, adultery, robbery and lying, participate in these things vicariously every week by willingly beholding them on TV and through videos.

King David declared, *"I will set no wicked thing before mine eyes"* (Psalm 101:3).

Scriptures condemn those acts, and judgment is pronounced against those who *"have pleasure in them that do them"* (Romans 1:32). In other words, those who enjoy watching others commit sin are themselves committing sin in their hearts.

There is a simple yet profound principle in Scripture that we are transformed into whom and what we worship. *"But we all, with open face beholding as in a glass the glory of the Lord, are changed into the same image from glory to glory, even as by the Spirit of the Lord"* (2 Corinthians 3:18).

As we turn our eyes upon Jesus and daily gaze at His pure and spotless life, we will find ourselves longing for that same purity. But in like manner, if we fill our minds with the wicked and frivolous programs that are so prevalent on TV, we will find that our hearts are constantly polluted with carnal cravings, our consciences will be seared, and we will lose our hunger and thirst for righteousness.

There is a dainty, bright-blue butterfly of less than an inch wingspread that has jewel-like gold spots on its wings. It is very lovely to behold, but it has a disgusting diet. Instead of soaring heavenward in sunlight or lighting upon flowers as it might, it descends to earth and feeds on dung.

There are millions of professed Christians who look like butterflies in church but who feed on filth at home as they revel in watching programs and videos that profane God's name and violate every commandment. If we ever hope to be pure in heart we must guard the avenues to our souls from these corrupting influences.

PURGING THE PURE GOLD

The most common use of the term "pure" in the Scriptures is in connection with gold. The phrase "pure gold" is found more than 45 times in the Bible. Gold is impervious to the ravages of time. It is not tarnished by air, water, nor most corrosives, and it can be melted down time and again without shedding any of its quality. In fact, a single ounce can be drawn out to make an unbroken wire 35 miles long or hammered into a sheet big enough to cover a tennis court! In the Bible, gold represents faith, hope, and love—the three purest principles that govern every true Christian (1 Corinthians 13:13). *"I counsel thee to buy of me gold tried in the fire, that thou mayest be rich"* (Revelation 3:18).

When gold is found in the earth, it is usually mixed with rock and soil that must be purged out, and this is accomplished with intense heat. Trouble, trials and pain are often the tools God uses to purify our hearts from earthly attachments.

"Wherein ye greatly rejoice, though now for a season, if need be, ye are in heaviness through manifold temptations: That the trial of your faith, being much more precious than of gold that perisheth, though it be tried with fire, might be found unto praise and honour and glory at the appearing of Jesus Christ" (1 Peter 1:6, 7).

"And he shall sit as a refiner and a purifier of silver: and he shall purify the sons of Levi, and purge them as gold and silver, that they may offer unto the LORD *an offering in righteousness"* (Malachi 3:3).

Our task is to pray for patience and faith that we might willingly submit to this refining process as we are purged for purity.

FOCUSED FOR HOME

As Christian pilgrims make the journey to the city with sure foundations, the enemy is ever seeking to turn our attention away from our splendid goal. After receiving the cleansing that Christ imparts, we can nurture this purity of heart only as we stay focused on Jesus and our marching orders to *"seek ye first the kingdom of God, and his righteousness"* (Matthew 6:33).

"Let us lay aside every weight, and the sin which doth so easily beset us, and let us run with patience the race that is set before us, Looking unto Jesus the author and finisher of our faith" (Hebrews 12:1, 2).

Here is where so many fail. They become distracted by the world and lose sight of their eternal objective. *"Demas hath forsaken me, having loved this present world"* (2 Timothy 4:10).

Paul said Jesus is coming for *"a glorious church, not having spot, or wrinkle, or any such thing; but that it should be holy and without blemish"* (Ephesians 5:27). The only way we can keep our garments clean is by keeping our attention directed to our Savior. *"And Jesus said unto him, No man, having put his hand to the plough, and looking back, is fit for the kingdom of God"* (Luke 9:62).

A man was visiting a friend in Massillon, Ohio, who had several homing pigeons in his back yard. The friend said, "See this white bird? She just flew the 500 miles from St. Louis non-stop!"

Stunned, the visitor said, "Non-stop! Now, how do you know? You weren't there. Did she tell you?"

He said, "Brother, there is a way to know—she came in clean. When she first arrived she had no maize, pollen, chaff, or mud on her feet, nothing on her to make me think she had stopped. She came in clean. She flew all day long, thinking only, 'I must get home; there will be somebody in the back yard waiting for me.'"

In the same manner, we get dirty when we become distracted from our goal. It is true that the blessed hope of Jesus' soon coming has a wondrous purifying influence on our attitudes and actions.

"We know that, when he shall appear, we shall be like him; for we shall see him as he is. And every man that hath this hope in him purifieth himself, even as he is pure" (1 John 3:2, 3).

Ultimately, it is love for Jesus that will motivate the true Christian to keep his garments unsullied from the world (Revelation 3:4). *"Who gave himself for us, that he might redeem us from all iniquity, and purify unto himself a peculiar people, zealous of good works"* (Titus 2:14).

Friend, are you longing for the peace and power that come as the fruit of a purified heart? You will find the cleansing blood of Jesus is only a prayer away.

A REAL SACRIFICE
CHAPTER TEN

An Amazing Fact: On May 21, 1946, Dr. Louis Slotin and seven other men were carrying out a dangerous experiment near Los Alamos, New Mexico. Their experiment included working with beryllium-coated spheres of plutonium, which become radioactive if they touch each other. Somehow the spheres were accidentally nudged a little too close together and the plutonium reached critical mass, producing a deadly upsurge of radioactivity. Slotin moved at once to save the others. With his bare hands, he pulled apart the radioactive spheres—but in so doing he exposed himself to an overwhelming dosage of radiation. Several days later he died, but not in vain. The other men recovered.

A young man named Jim Elliot was one of five missionaries murdered in the jungles of Ecuador while attempting to take the gospel to the Auca Indians. All five men were armed with guns, yet they allowed themselves to be speared to death by the hostile tribe because they had resolved not to shoot any natives—even in self-defense.

Later, Elliot's wife and daughter returned to the Auca Indians along with the sister of Nate Saint, who also died in the massacre. Together these ladies brought the tribe to the knowledge of Jesus Christ. Gikita, the Auca who led the attack against the five missionaries, testified: "God says now you are forgiven. And I know I'm forgiven for all these spearings. I'm going to meet Nate Saint in heaven someday. And we'll just wrap our arms around each other and be happy."

Elliot once said, "He is no fool to give what he cannot keep to gain what he cannot lose." He was doubtless referring to the words of Jesus, who declared, *"He that findeth his life shall lose it: and he that loseth his life for my sake shall find it"* (Matthew 10:39).

To make a real sacrifice is in many ways the very essence of the gospel. Jesus demonstrated this perfectly when He left the courts of glory, the adoration of the angels, and the perfect vitality of an infinite body to take on the form of a feeble human.

Jesus said in John 20:21, *"As my Father hath sent me, even so send I you."* He came into the world as the supreme sacrifice, and now He asks His followers to likewise become living sacrifices. Let's find out exactly what this means and what we can do to make a real sacrifice that is pleasing to Him.

IT'S COSTLY

The first characteristic of a real sacrifice is that it costs the giver something. We can find scriptural evidence for this principle by comparing stories involving Israel's first two kings.

The Bible reveals in 1 Samuel 15 that King Saul did not have a correct concept of sacrifice. Before attacking the Amalekites, he was instructed by the Lord to completely annihilate the people, including their animals and everything they owned. However, in the battle, Saul was unwilling to destroy the Amalekite king or the best-looking cattle.

As he returned from the slaughter herding goats, sheep and oxen, the prophet Samuel met Saul and expressed his keen disappointment. *"You were instructed to completely destroy these people, who have been plaguing you for years,"* he said. *"They and their animals were to be obliterated."*

Unrepentant, King Saul said to Samuel: *"I have obeyed the voice of the LORD, and gone on the mission on which the LORD sent me, and brought back Agag king of Amalek; I have utterly destroyed the Amalekites. But the people took of the plunder, sheep and oxen, the best of the things which should have been utterly destroyed, to sacrifice to the LORD your God in Gilgal"* (verses 20–21, NKJV).

Saul's platitudes about planning to sacrifice the animals they had spared sound very pious on the surface. However, is stealing something from someone else to give it as a offering truly a sacrifice? No, indeed!

Unlike Saul, King David understood this concept. After a plague decimated 70,000 men of Israel, the prophet Gad told David to offer a sacrifice on the threshing floor of Ornan the Jubusite (1 Chronicles 21:18). When Ornan offered to give it to the king, David refused, saying, *"No, but I will surely buy it for the full price, for I will not take what is yours for the* Lord, *nor offer burnt offerings with that which costs me nothing"* (verse 24, NKJV). A sacrifice is not a sacrifice if it demands no personal cost when you give it.

It's Inconvenient

A nother characteristic of a true sacrifice is that it is seldom convenient. I don't know about you, but I am selfish, and I must confess that putting other people above my own selfish desires is a challenge I face every day.

I am ashamed to admit that every now and then, I feel put out when my wife Karen asks me to watch our children. It seems I've always got so much to do. Besides, kids are not always as engaging as adults and they don't like to play the same games I like to play. They also require a lot of attention.

Then I heard about the emperor penguin. The female, at the coldest part of the polar winter, lays one egg and then gives it to the male. He jostles it up on top of his feet and covers it with the extra layers of fat from his belly to keep it warm. Then he stands still and incubates the egg for two months without going to eat. Talk about inconvenience! Why do the male emperor penguins do it? Perhaps they know that making this sacrifice is the only way to create new life.

In the same way, spreading the gospel sometimes requires us to sacrifice our convenience so that others might live. A real sacrifice will challenge our inherent selfishness.

It Represents Our Best

A third important characteristic of genuine sacrifice is that it must represent our best. The Old Testament states repeatedly that all offerings presented to the Lord were to be without blemish (Exodus 12:5). They were to be flawless, healthy specimens to symbolize the spotless coming Messiah.

Unfortunately, after a time, the children of Israel began to reason: "The priest is going to kill this animal as soon as I take it to the temple. Why should I take my best and healthiest, which I could use for breeding, when I've got a sick one here that I could easily do without? It's missing one eye and it's gimpy and old, but what difference does that make? It's going die to anyway." So they ignored God's command to offer lambs, goats and oxen without blemish and instead gave the lame and the blind as offerings.

Malachi 1:8 reveals what God thought of their disobedience. He asks: *"'And when you offer the blind as a sacrifice, is it not evil? And when you offer the lame and sick, is it not evil? Offer it then to your governor! Would he be pleased with you? Would he accept you favorably?' says the LORD of hosts"* (NKJV).

We often do to God what we would never do to each other. For instance, most of us would never dream of showing up at the governor's house for dinner dressed like we're going to the beach. Yet when we come to the Lord's house, we sometimes act like we're going to a picnic and forget that He is the exalted King of the universe. Or when the offering plate comes by in church, we give God a small tip—a lame sacrifice. Some of us tip waiters and waitresses better than we "tip" the Lord for His goodness and mercy.

I've fallen into this trap myself. Just before the offering plate went by one Sabbath, I reached into my wallet and found a very old $20 bill alongside a brand new $20 bill. My old $20 was all crumpled up, and as I reached for it I thought, "Oh, it's just an offering." Right then and there the Lord said to me: "You're going to give Me the old one? Give Me the pretty one." That was a little thing, yet it's so typical of our tendency to give God the leftovers and call it a sacrifice.

GIVING YOUR TIME

There are several specific areas in which Christians are called to sacrifice. The first has to do with time. To be a true Christian, you must give your time to God.

Albert Schweitzer, an internationally known concert organist whose musical career lasted well into his eighties, came under great conviction at age 21 that he must give his life to the Lord. He then wrote a covenant, stating that "for nine years I intend to devote myself to the study of music, theology, and medicine, then I will spend the rest of my life, God willing, serving humankind."

In 1913, after obtaining his doctorate in philosophy and a medical degree, Schweitzer went to the equator and founded a hospital at Lambarene in French Equatorial Africa. He lived there with his wife for the majority of his life, serving God as a surgeon, pastor, village administrator, and prolific theological writer. With the money he received from winning the 1953 Nobel Peace Prize, he started a leprosarium.

By 1960, the jungle hospital in Lambarene had expanded to more than 70 buildings that could accommodate 500 patients. When Schweitzer died at age 90, he was buried on the hospital grounds.

I believe that because this man dedicated his time to serving the Lord, God honored him with a long life. Schweitzer spent about 50 years serving people in the very humble setting of an African mission hospital. That's a real sacrifice.

GIVING OF YOUR RESOURCES

Being a Christian requires a real sacrifice of your means. Many of us give to the Lord, but we don't give sacrificially.

Think of the widow in the Bible who put her last two cents into the offering box (Mark 12:42–44). That was a real sacrifice, which is why Jesus called attention to it. It wasn't the amount of money that mattered. God doesn't care about the money; He owns everything already (Psalm 50:12). It was the amount of sacrifice that moved the Lord to draw attention to this widow, who, despite her poverty, gave everything she had out of her deep love for the Lord.

When most of us give an offering, we go home in the same car, wearing the same clothes, sleeping in the same bed with the same pillow, and eating all of the same food. In other words, we don't really feel any tangible vacuum. A genuine sacrifice, in which we give something and immediately feel the loss, is pretty rare these days.

We sometimes forget that the offerings that we give come back to us in various forms. I don't think a Christian should make sacrifices just because he believes it's going to come back, but it is a fact that it does come back. The Bible promises, *"Give and it will be given to you: good measure, pressed down, shaken together, and running over will be put into your bosom. For with the same measure that you use, it will be measured back to you"* (Luke 6:38, NKJV).

I know a very successful businessman who gives up to half of his income for a worthy project, and I've never seen somebody who is followed by so many blessings. I think the Lord keeps blessing him with incredible opportunities and contracts because he gives until it hurts. He can be trusted with success. Many of us never realize that kind of blessing because we're afraid to give sacrificially.

GIVING UP YOUR RIGHTS

Christians are also sometimes called on to sacrifice their rights. Do you remember the Bible story in which Elisha the prophet led the entire Syrian army into the hands of the king of Israel (2 Kings 6:18–23)? Ready to execute this army that has been surrounded by his forces, the Israelite king asked Elisha: *"Shall I smite them? Shall I smite them?"*

The prophet's response must have astounded the eager monarch. The Syrians had been trying to ambush and assassinate the king. At last the king had them where he wanted them, but to his surprise, Elisha told him to sacrifice his right for revenge and, instead, feed his enemies and let them go.

Sacrificing our rights can be a struggle. I feel this most keenly whenever I'm driving, because I don't appreciate it when other drivers violate my rights. For example, I get annoyed when people race ahead while traffic is merging instead of taking turns and alternating. They drive down the shoulder and try to squeeze in front of the lead car, as if they were more important than everyone else.

I'm very competitive, so if I see someone trying to squeeze in when they ought to have merged a half-mile back, my natural reaction is to think, "You have no right to squeeze in here." So I'll try to keep my car right on the brake lights of the car ahead of me so that person can't get in.

Then Jesus starts to deal with me. He says: "Doug, you've done the very same thing before. Let the car get in front of you. Sacrifice your right." I may not always like it, but I must admit that with so little observable Christianity in the world, the least I can do is preach through my driving.

When we sacrifice our rights, we display the characteristics of Christ.

GIVING SOMEONE ELSE CREDIT

It is often said that there is no limit to what can be accomplished if we're not worried about who gets the credit. This is true in the church as well as in the world. Real Christians are willing to sacrifice the credit they deserve.

Perhaps you remember the story of Gideon, who under the power of God defeated the Midianite army with just 300 men (Judges 7:1–25). Afterward, the men of Ephraim were outraged that they were not part of the battle, and they wanted to fight with Gideon. However, he was able to avoid what seemed a certain battle against his countrymen by telling them, "Oh, but you've managed to capture the two princes and you won the battle" (see Judges 8:3). He gave the Ephraimites credit for winning the battle against the Midianites, even though they didn't deserve it. Gideon saved the day by sacrificing credit for the great victory.

I also like the story in which Joseph sacrificed an opportunity to take credit for interpreting the Egyptian monarch's dream. *"It is not in me: God shall give Pharaoh an answer of peace"* (Genesis 41:16). Daniel did the same thing when he told the king of Babylon, *"There is a God in heaven who reveals secrets, and He has made known to King Nebuchadnezzar what will be in the latter days"* (Daniel 2:28, NKJV). If we have God's Spirit dwelling in us, we too will be willing to sacrifice an opportunity to hog the credit.

GIVING UP SECURITY

Deciding to serve the Lord may also require us to sacrifice earthly security. Christians need to live by faith, which means that our trust is not in a bank or a job, but in the Lord.

When families go to the mission field, they usually sacrifice the security of suburban America—with its gated communities, auto alarms and video cameras. However, I'm convinced that if we sacrifice our security to do the will of God, we will be safer in the midst of the most dangerous jungle than if we were surrounded by police escorts yet living outside the will of God. Being in God's will is, without a doubt, the most secure place on earth.

Love, which is the essence of being a Christian, involves great risk. We are commanded not only to love God, but also to love our neighbors as ourselves (Mark 12:30, 31). This, of course, is not easy.

C.S. Lewis made some profound statements relating to this subject in his book The Four Loves. He wrote: "To love at all is to be vulnerable. Love anything, and your heart will certainly be wrung and possibly be broken. If you want to make sure of keeping it intact, you must give your heart to no one, not even to an animal. Wrap it carefully round with hobbies and little luxuries; avoid all entanglements; lock it up safe in the casket or coffin of your selfishness. But in that casket—safe, dark, motionless, airless—it will change. It will not be broken; it will become unbreakable, impenetrable, irredeemable."

To be true Christians, we must sacrifice the idea that we're never going to be hurt, wounded, or persecuted. The only place outside of heaven where you can be perfectly secure from all dangers of love is hell.

GIVING YOUR LIFE

Of course, the ultimate sacrifice a person can make is to sacrifice his life. John 15:13 says, *"Greater love hath no man than this, that a man lay down his life for his friends."*

Inspired by the great love God demonstrated for us in sacrificing His Son, James Calvert went to the Fiji islands as a Christian missionary. As the ship captain was lowering Calvert and his small team onto the islands, which were renowned for what the cannibals had done to other missionaries before them, the man said: "You realize this is suicide. Aren't you afraid?"

The missionary replied: "No, we're not afraid of dying. I died long ago."

When you come to the Lord, you are crucified with Christ (Galatians 2:20). And if you have really been crucified with Christ, then nothing can be considered a sacrifice because you've already willed all of your assets to God. Philippians 1:21 says, *"For to me to live is Christ, and to die is gain."*

Christian pioneer David Livingstone wrote: "People talk of the sacrifice I have made in spending so much of my life in Africa. Can that be called a sacrifice which is simply paid back as a small part of the great debt owing to our God, which we can never repay? Is that a sacrifice which brings its own blest reward in healthful activity, the consciousness of doing good, peace of mind, and a bright hope of a glorious destiny hereafter? Away with the word in such a view, and with such a thought! It is emphatically no sacrifice. Say rather it is a privilege."

Livingstone spent 30 years in Africa, exploring one-third of the continent and taking the gospel to those who had never heard the name of Christ. Often plagued with fever and dysentery, he died on his knees in prayer. Yet he said: "I never made a sacrifice. Of this we ought not to talk, when we remember the great sacrifice which He made who left His Father's throne on high to give Himself for us."

The apostle Paul challenged believers: *"I beseech you therefore, brethren, by the mercies of God, that ye present your bodies a living sacrifice, holy, acceptable unto God, which is your reasonable service. And be not conformed to this world: but be ye transformed by the renewing of your mind, that ye may prove what is that good, and acceptable, and perfect, will of God"* (Romans 12:1–2).

TWO MORE GREAT STORIES OF SACRIFICE

Many years ago, a Chinese Christian named Lough Fook learned that some of his comrades were working as unskilled laborers in South African mines. Most were Buddhists, and he wanted to share Christ with them. They lived in shantytowns and worked all day long under terribly pathetic conditions, without hope of everlasting life. So Lough Fook sold himself into slavery to work in these mines and preach the gospel to them. As a result of his sacrifice, nearly 200 of his countrymen came to Christ in the five years before he died in the mine. Giving your life like that to serve others is a real sacrifice.

Declared an "American Hero" in 1985 by former U.S. President Ronald Reagan, Clara Hale was devoted to nurturing drug-addicted children. Here is her story:

After her husband died, Clara started cleaning houses during the day and working at a local theater at night to support her family. Soon convinced that her three children were not being properly supervised at daycare, she decided to work at home, caring for her own children as well as those whose mothers couldn't or wouldn't care for them. Over the next 28 years, "Mother Hale" made an impact on thousands of lives.

When problems related to drug abuse dramatically increased in Harlem, Clara's family urged her to take action. Soon she had 22 babies of heroin-addicted women in her apartment. Although she had no prior knowledge about caring for drug-addicted infants, she and her daughter nurtured the babies and the mothers. She helped to establish the Hale House, a hospital and childcare facility that was the first in the United States specifically designed to deal with babies who were born addicted to illegal drugs. Hale House became the "Center for the Promotion of Human Potential" in 1975.

During her life, Mother Hale cared for more than 500 children and received both national and international recognition for her sacrificial work. She died in 1993, but she will not soon be forgotten.

REMEMBERING REVERENCE
CHAPTER ELEVEN

An Amazing Fact: Marco Polo reports that the Great Kublai Khan of China was enormously respected. Anybody coming within 500 meters from him had to lower his voice and behave humbly. If someone had an invitation to the palace, he had to take off his shoes and put on white leather slippers before entering the palace. If he wished to spit, he had to take with him a small covered vessel. Forgetting to respect the Great Khan could quickly result in death from the hands of one of his 10,000 bodyguards!

SOMETHING TO LEARN

During a recent trip to Chile, a friend took me to visit some old churches. Virtually all the towns in Latin America are laid out with a plaza in the middle with a church standing as a central focus of that town square. Once inside these mini-cathedrals, I was amazed how quickly the atmosphere transitioned away from the noisy streets with the commotion of traffic and flea market vendors. Inside the church, I was met with an awesome silence. Sometimes only a handful of people would be praying, but they still maintained an air of extraordinary reverence.

In these churches, they have a deep concept of God as holy. God is to be revered; you are to come trembling before His presence. I wonder if some Protestant churches are losing an important aspect of real Christian worship by ignoring the issue of reverence. I believe there's a special message of reverence that God wants to go to the world in the last days.

AN IMPORTANT END-TIME MESSAGE

In Revelation 14:7, we hear the first of the three angels' messages; it is a special admonition to *"Fear God, and give glory to him; for the hour of his judgment is come."*

We often understand the word "fear" in terms of terror—to be afraid. But the word used here as "fear" is the Greek "phobeo" (the root word of phobia.) It doesn't mean only to be afraid of something—like claustrophobia or some other phobia. This word also translates, according to *Strong's Concordance*, as "to be in awe of, to revere, to fear exceedingly and to reverence."

I believe God is telling us that in the last days, the church is to teach the world to revere Him—to be in awe of their Creator. But to a great extent, the church has lost this attitude of reverence, which is also defined as "a feeling of profound awe, respect, often love, veneration, honor." The Bible tells us that it does not come naturally to the proud, fallen hearts of man. Humans need to be taught reverence for sacred things. So let's address some areas where we as Christians can better demonstrate and express our reverence for God. Titus 2:1–7 says: *"But as for you, speak the things which are proper for sound doctrine: that the older men be sober, **reverent**, temperate, sound in faith, in love, in patience; the older women likewise, that they be **reverent in behavior**... Likewise, exhort the young men to... [show] integrity, **reverence**"* (NKJV, emphasis added). It is obvious from this Scripture that God wants us to be more reverent, more humble, and show more respect to Him and others.

REVERENCE IS HAPPINESS AND STRENGTH

"*For thou shalt worship no other god: for the LORD, whose name is Jealous, is a jealous God"* (Exodus 34:14).

Worship is a central theme in the Bible. It's very important to exhibit reverence during worship; it demonstrates your concept of the level of greatness of the one being worshiped. The devil hates when we revere God. He wants us to jeer and be sarcastic or indifferent regarding holy things—the opposite of reverence. If we do not make a conscious effort in remembering reverence, Satan is going to do everything he can to chisel away at the foundation of our worship, which is a sense of awe and respect for God and His greatness.

Yet reverence is not something that should make you sad or somber. Proverbs 28:14 says, *"Happy is the man who is always reverent"* (NKJV). Isn't that good news? Being reverent isn't supposed to cast a cloud on your worship experience. It's supposed to enhance the true happiness of your worship experience.

"Reverence is a sign of strength," someone said. "Irreverence is a sure indication of weakness. No man will rise high who jeers at sacred things. Real strength can be verified in reverence." This reverent strength can be demonstrated in many ways.

WHAT'S IN A NAME?

"Let them praise thy great and terrible name; for it is holy" (Psalm 99:3).

First, let's consider this foremost sign of reverence: God's name. Psalm 111:9 says, "Holy and reverend is his name." I once had a meeting with ministers from various denominations, and I was given a nametag that said, "Reverend Batchelor." That's more like an oxymoron, isn't it? I felt really uncomfortable with it. I remembered Psalm 111 and felt convicted, so later I flipped my nametag over and wrote "Pastor Doug." That sounded more like where I belong on the scale of things.

In recent years, great prominence has been placed on Jesus as our Friend. And He is our Friend: "Ye are my friends, if ye do whatsoever I command you" (John 15:14). But He's also our Creator and King. We must not forget that. I believe this overemphasis of Jesus as our casual buddy has diminished our sense of awe and veneration for Him. I believe that angels are sometimes grieved by the casual and glib way some Christians speak of God.

Taking God's name in vain is a sure sign of irreverence. I have a Russian friend who, during World War II, served in Japan as a translator. He literally spoke for the Emperor when reading messages. He said, "When I spoke Japanese, I spoke as they did. But whenever I spoke for the Emperor, I used a different voice." They actually trained him to use that voice, which was supposed to sound like a god speaking. In the same way, we should never say the name of God in jest or a flippant manner.

God's name should always be spoken with solemnity on our lips—for He is the highest Monarch in all of the cosmos. We need to revere His name. The Levites were chosen as the priests of God because when other Jews worshiped the golden calf, Levi's family refused to because they revered the name of God. *"My covenant was with him, one of life and peace, And I gave them to him that he might fear Me; So he feared Me and was reverent before My name"* (Malachi 2:5 NKJV).

Augustine said, "God is not greater if you reverence Him, but you are greater if you serve Him." Reverencing God's name doesn't make God more holy—He's great no matter what you say or think. But you are greater when you revere His name.

GOD'S WORD

"**F**or thou hast magnified thy word above all thy name" (Psalm 138:2).

Imagine that! This Scripture says God Himself exalts His Word above His name. So we need to treat the Bible, His Word, with particular reverence. I've watched preachers shake, pound, and throw their Bibles like some puny pulpit prop when they preach. The Bible isn't just some Christian "policy book." It's a sacred revelation from God.

At home, the Bible should be placed somewhere where you won't just pile things on it. Would you do that with a rare photograph of someone you love? Of course not! The Bible is much the same: It's a sacred love letter from God to us. During family worship, we demonstrate to our children a reverence for God's Word. We take time every day to read from the Bible.

In the church I pastor, we stand during the Scripture reading. The reason for this is found in Nehemiah 8:5; when Ezra opens the book in the sight of all the people, they all stand up out of respect for the sacred Word. You stand when you greet a person of honor; it's a gesture of respect and esteem. So when God is getting ready to speak, should we show Him any less honor?

The Bible is a holy book; its words are precious. They should be spoken clearly and accurately. Remember that Revelation pronounces a curse upon anyone who alters His Word (Revelation 22:18, 19).

Consider also how God placed ultimate respect on His Word when He delivered the Ten Commandments to His people. They were set in a golden safe, the ark, in the center of the temple called the holy of Holies. In fact, each of the Ten Commandments addresses reverence. Think about it: They deal with respect for God's position and Person, His name, His Sabbath day, for parents and for life, marriage, truth, and property.

God's message to us in the Bible is full of reverence, so let's show His Word the kind of reverence that He expects and deserves from His creation.

SHOWING HONOR IN WORSHIP

" *God is greatly to be feared in the assembly of the saints*" (Psalm 89:7).

In the conversion experience of Isaiah described in Chapter 6:1–8, he sees God seated in His temple in regal holiness, and the house shakes with the voice of God. Six-winged seraphim hover around the throne of God, covering their faces and feet and perpetually singing *"Holy, holy, holy."* (Like that wonderful hymn!) Someone once suggested that "holy" is sung once for the Father, a "holy" for the Son, and a "holy" for the Holy Ghost. Whenever God says something three times in the Bible, He is emphasizing its eternal quality. When beholding this awesome scene, Isaiah responded by falling to the floor before the Lord, saying, *"Woe is me! I am undone."* Please don't miss this truth that a picture of the holiness of God brought about the conversion and the call of the prophet Isaiah! We diminish these converting powers of our services when we are irreverent in worship. Daniel and the apostle John also fell down like Isaiah when God appeared to them in visions. They revered God in their worship.

What would happen if God Almighty suddenly appeared before you right now? Would you survive? He said to Moses, *"No man can see my face and live,"* which is why He put Moses in the cleft of the rock. He covered Moses' eyes with His hands so he couldn't see God's face. The Bible says man will someday see God the Father, but right now in our impure condition, we can't endure His blazing glory. This is the most glorious, powerful, awesome Being. When we come together to worship Him, there should be a sense of awe in His presence.

Reverence during worship means our posture and conduct too.

Adults should sit up in church, and not sit with their feet up on the pew or slouching like our skeletons have been removed.

I also believe we should be respectful in our attire. Now I'm not saying you need expensive clothes to show reverence—the Bible doesn't teach that. But the Bible does say that we should come before the Lord clean. When giving His Law, God told the people, *"Wash your clothes before you meet with the LORD."* Furthermore, if we have good clothing—wear your best for God. Some people wear a suit through the week, yet they come to church in their gym clothes. If that's all you have that's fine, but don't give God the leftovers. Don't be more respectful for your employer than you are for your Creator.

There's a real danger that unless we remind ourselves of this awe, our sense of reverence can evaporate. How you worship God says volumes about who you think He is. If we worship God in a disrespectful manner, we send a message to unbelievers of a diminished concept of God's greatness. Josephus said in his writings, "The Jewish temple was held in reverence by nations from all over the earth." You can tell a lot about people by how they take care of their houses, can't you? A front yard can reveal much about the family that lives inside.

THE SOUND OF SILENCE

"**W**alk *prudently when you go to the house of God; and draw near to hear rather than to give the sacrifice of fools, for they do not know that they do evil. Do not be rash with your mouth, And let not your heart utter anything hastily before God. For God is in heaven, and you on earth; Therefore let your words be few"* (Ecclesiastes 5:1, 2 NKJV).

There are many ways reverence in worship can be demonstrated through quiet contemplation and listening. For instance, the words we say in church should be few and carefully chosen. Children should be taught to sit quietly. (I've got a litter of kids; I know it's a challenge!) People shouldn't blurt out or talk loudly in times of solemn assembly. You know, an important sign of intelligence is learning when to speak and when to be quiet. *"But the LORD is in his holy temple. Let all the earth keep silence before him"* (Habakkuk 2:20).

Sometimes while the Word of God is being proclaimed, I think the devil deliberately creates a disturbance through loud children and restless teens to detract from our sense of reverence during worship. How can it not distract when a cell phone rings or someone starts to snore! It's offensive when adults are gabbing during the sacred service in God's holy place. We need to remain humble and quiet during worship, because this is how we respect our teachers in school and our judges in court. Why would we do less for God?

In Prayer

"O come, let us worship and bow down: let us kneel before the LORD our maker" (Psalm 95:6).

It is not necessary to always kneel when you are praying. Nehemiah prayed while working, and Peter prayed while swimming. Indeed, we are to *"Pray without ceasing"* (1 Thessalonians 5:17). We'd be crawling on our knees wherever we went! But I also think that at the start of formal worship service, and especially in your personal devotions, if you're physically able, you should kneel before God. Of course, some people cannot kneel because of knee or back problems. And sometimes when we get older, once we get down we can't get back up very easily. God knows that. He's a loving God. God is more interested in the posture of your heart than your body. But if you're able, it's appropriate to get down before God. Posture represents a sign of reverence, an attitude of worship. If not before Him, then whom?

And reverence in prayer needs to be taught. In the Batchelor family, sometimes before prayer, the kids are playing with their toys. We say, "Put the toys down when we pray." We ask them to fold their hands, even though the Bible doesn't command us to do that. But you know what? They're less inclined to fiddle with their siblings or toys when their hands are folded. So there's some good theology in that custom.

We also ask them to close their eyes. The Bible doesn't say you have to close your eyes. When you get older, you can pray with your eyes open. I do sometimes. You might even pray while looking up. The Bible talks about that. But when they're little and so stimulated visually, they can be easily distracted. We'll often hear, "Mom, Nathan's eyes are open." And we're thinking, "Well, Stephen, how did you know? Your eyes must have been open too." And then sometimes I catch myself: I'll be peeking at them to see if their eyes are open, and they're peeking at me to see if I'm peeking at them! This is all part of the learning process, but you have to teach it. It's disrespectful when someone is speaking to you and you are not paying attention. Likewise, in prayer, when communing with God we should keep focused.

REMEMBERING THE HOLY SABBATH DAY

"R*emember the sabbath day, to keep it holy*" (Exodus 20:8).

God calls only a few things holy; those things should absolutely be revered. The Sabbath is one of these very holy dimensions of worship to God. It's not a day for common conversation or activity.

Through the week, my mind is always racing with work that needs to be done around our house. But on the Sabbath, I say "God, it's your Sabbath now. Help my mind stay on sacred things." If you pray this, the Holy Spirit will help you. And whenever I catch my mind starting to drift away to the next construction or repair project, the Holy Spirit will say, "Doug, it's the Sabbath." I respond, "Thank you, Lord. I don't have to worry about those things now." Our minds need to rest, and to keep the Sabbath holy in your mind is where it all begins.

Keeping reverence for Sabbath is also a matter of the way we spend our time and money. The Bible says we should prepare our food and other needs in advance so that we don't scurry and hustle about on the Sabbath. In Exodus 16:23, God rained down the bread from heaven for six days, but He stopped on the Sabbath. Why? He set a precedent for gathering food in advance. "*Tomorrow is a Sabbath rest, a holy Sabbath to the* LORD. *Bake what you will bake today, and boil what you will boil; and lay up for yourselves and all that remains, to be kept until morning*" (NKJV).

We should also keep the Sabbath as a sign of reverence to others. We shouldn't go out to eat on the Sabbath and hire others to work on a day when we know God wants His people to be an example to others. Having this kind of reverence is a powerful witness. Many like to argue specific points on what is permissible on the Sabbath; I believe when in doubt, don't do anything you even think might dishonor God. Pray, and God will provide the answer.

Conclusion

" *And what shall I more say? for the time would fail me to tell*" (Hebrews 11:32).

If space permitted, I could talk in detail about the lost reverence for life that is seen in the insensitive way the secular world views abortion and euthanasia—or reverence for creation that has been lost to the polluters and litterbugs. I could also address reverence for our bodies that would revolutionize our thinking in everything from healthful living to pornography. And I could also discuss the reverence needed in our giving that would influence better offerings and prevent the looted tithe so many bring to God. The list is a long one, and it would all be about reverence! So remember that in every thing given by our God, be reverent and respectful for what it is: a holy gift. People pay big bucks to go to the symphony. They dress up in formal clothing. They shut the doors and turn off cell phones before the concert begins. Perhaps they think Mozart's musical creations are so beautiful that they feel they owe this respect. But why are we doing this increasingly less for the Almighty?

Are we losing this concept of what is truly great and awesome? Let me tell you, God is awesome! Have you ever had one of those epiphanies where suddenly you're reminded with the reality of God—like something in His creation that makes you go "Wow!" In Chile, I visited some huge volcanoes high in the Andes Mountains. Steam puffed out from these majestic, beautiful snow-capped peaks. And it is breathtaking. Seeing that splendor pulled back the veil and helped me glimpse the greatness of God, the Creator of the infinite cosmos. And I thought, "This is the God who loves me. Who died to save me!"

Would you like to have a closer relationship with Jesus? Do you want to have a joyful experience with Him both here and when He returns? Well then, don't forget that "Happy is the man who is always reverent." I believe if many of us would rediscover and experience a revival in our reverence, God will meet us in a special way. I truly believe that when we remember reverence, it will invite the angels into our homes and churches and seal God's throne in our hearts.

Reviving Dry Bones
Chapter Twelve

An Amazing Fact: Not all cemeteries keep the dearly departed underground. A church in Rome, called "Santa Maria della Immaculata Concezione," built in 1626, houses one of the most interesting crypts in the world. The tomb is called the "Cemetery dei Cappuccini," or "Cemetery of Capuchins." However, the remains of it's 4,000 monks are not buried; instead, they are on display—as lamp stands made of fibulae, as intricate frescoes of scapulae and vertebrae, and as hanging chandeliers made of more delicate bones. And similarly in Faro, Portugal, a tiny chapel behind an 18th century church has actually been built with nothing but bones and a little cement!

Most people associate the book of Ezekiel with one of two things: God's chariot with the "wheel in the middle of a wheel," or the dry bones that come back to life. Both of these visions have inspired several lively songs, but rarely are they the subject of practical or serious Bible study.

Here, I want to focus on the vision of the valley of dry bones, found in Ezekiel 37:1–14, because we can learn many profound things from this fascinating passage of Scripture.

The book of Ezekiel was written by the prophet bearing the same name, which means "God will strengthen." A Hebrew from the tribe of Levi, he was among the elite of Judah who were captured by Nebuchadnezzar and carried away to Babylon. Ezekiel prophesied between the years 600 and 570 BC and was a contemporary of the prophet Daniel. Some scholars believe that his reference in the very first verse of the book to "the thirtieth year" was probably an indication of his age. If so, that means Ezekiel would have been only 25 years old at the time he was forced to leave his homeland. Thirty was also the age when a priest could begin to minister (Numbers 4:3). It was at age 30 that Jesus began His ministry, Joseph began to rule over Egypt, and David began his reign.

This fascinating prophecy of dry bones in Ezekiel has something for every body. (Pardon the pun.) First of all, he was speaking primarily to his fellow captives among the children of Israel. By this time in history, the 10 tribes of Israel had been so widely scattered among the surrounding nations that they seemed all but lost as a people. The tribes of Judah, Benjamin and Levi had just been conquered and carried away captive to Babylon. It looked as if their national identity was forever gone and they would never again return to their Promised Land. Hence, one purpose of this vision was to inspire them with hope that God would someday revive them as a nation.

In addition, this prophecy speaks about what God will do for spiritual Israel, which is the church today. An obvious theme of the vision is that God can resurrect dry bones—that He can give literal life to that which is dead and inanimate. It is a message that He can revive His people and turn them into a mighty army.

Last of all, it speaks to us individually. No matter how dried up and worthless we may feel, or how dead in trespasses and sins, God can restore us to life through His Word and Spirit.

ANKLE-DEEP IN BONES

E zekiel begins his account with these words: *"The hand of the LORD was upon me, and carried me out in the spirit of the LORD, and set me down in the midst of the valley which was full of bones"* (Ezekiel 37:1).

Picture the scene for a moment: Ezekiel was carried off in the Spirit and taken to an obscure valley. The Promised Land is home to the lowest spot on earth. Located down below the Jordan Valley, near the Dead Sea, this valley is more than 1,300 feet below sea level. Perhaps Ezekiel was taken in vision down to this very low and very hot area, where Sodom and Gomorrah used to stand.

Everywhere, on every side, were dead men's bleached bones. Talk about Death Valley! In this macabre vision, Ezekiel was surrounded with a countless number of bleaching bones from this slain multitude.

Now keep in mind that when an army was defeated in battle in Bible times, the victorious soldiers would often strip the valuables from the slain and then leave their enemies' bodies unburied. In remote places where there had been serious battles, skeletons sometimes remained for years afterward, until the beasts of carrion completely scattered the bones or they surrendered to the elements. This image of a valley covered with bones was not merely an abstract concept. Ezekiel lived at a time when one could find literal valleys of bones—places where the slain enemy had been overwhelmed and there was no one to bury them. In the Bible, a corpse not properly buried was considered to be accursed by God.

This image also has a lot of relevance for us. The Bible tells us that just after the Lord comes, the surface of the earth will remain convoluted and destroyed for 1,000 years. The earth will look like a wilderness strewn with the corpses of the lost. Cities will be broken down, and nobody will be there to lament, to mourn, or to bury the dead. *"And the slain of the LORD shall be at that day from one end of the earth even unto the other end of the earth,"* says Jeremiah 25:33. This entire world is going to be a dark valley of dry bones that will someday come to life for judgment.

Ezekiel was not only a prophet of God, he was also a priest. The poor guy was placed in the midst of this valley of bones, and he said that the Lord *"caused me to pass by them"* (verse 2). Can you imagine walking around ankle-deep in the bones of dead men? It might have been a dog's dream come true, but it likely made the prophet extremely uncomfortable. To touch a dead body would render anybody, but especially a priest, unclean. How objectionable it must have been for Ezekiel to be placed, even in vision, in this gruesome field of death!

NEW LIFE TO THE LIFELESS

The Bible says these bones were *"very dry"* (verse 2). There wasn't any hope of life.

I understand that while doing some excavating in an ancient peat bog in England, a team of archaeologists found some very small lily seeds, which they planted. Although scientists estimate that those seeds had been there for thousands of years, they sprouted and produced a lily. There's nothing else like it in the world today because that particular plant had at some point become extinct. Yet because life was somehow preserved in that seed, the flower could live again.

However, you can't stick a dry bone in water and expect it to come back to life. Even if you fertilized it and watered it for a hundred years, it would never live again. So these "very dry" bones symbolized a situation that looked completely hopeless.

Remember that this vision was given as a lesson not only for a nation or for the church, but also for us as individuals. These dry bones represent people. The Bible says, *"He that hath the Son hath life; and he that hath not the Son of God hath not life"* (1 John 5:12). If a person does not have Jesus, his bones are bleached, white and dry. Spiritually speaking, he has no life.

Just as water brings the parched earth to life, God's Word and living water of His Spirit will bring dry souls new life. Isaiah 44:3 says, *"For I will pour water upon him that is thirsty, and floods upon the dry ground: I will pour my spirit upon thy seed, and my blessing upon thine offspring."*

Ephesians 2:1 says, *"And you hath he quickened [revived], who were dead in trespasses and sins."* If sin still reigns in our lives, if we're still controlled by a life of sin, then we're spiritually dead. We are as good as dry bones. Thankfully, the hope in this story is that God can revive dry bones.

"For this my son was dead," the father said of the prodigal son, *"and is alive again; he was lost, and is found"* (Luke 15:24). When was the rebellious son dead? When he was out living a riotous life. Spiritually he was as dead as a dry mummy, but then God brought him to his knees and restored him to his senses.

Mission Possible!

I n the vision, God asked Ezekiel a question. He said, *"Son of man, can these bones live?"*

The prophet replied, *"O Lord God, thou knowest"* (verse 3).

God knows everything. He doesn't ask us questions because He's been stumped; He asks to get us to think. Just as the ancient philosopher Socrates used to teach by asking questions, so too God asks people questions to arouse their thought processes and get them to analyze the situation. *"Come now, and let us reason together, saith the* LORD*"* (Isaiah 1:18).

If Ezekiel had responded to God's question based on the evidence of his senses, he would have answered "no." Dead, dry bones cannot come back to life.

If you were the first to the scene of an accident and you saw somebody lying motionless on the ground, you might think, "Perhaps there's hope." You would probably even do a little CPR to try to revive the person. But if you saw a skeleton lying in the road, you wouldn't even consider giving it mouth-to-mouth resuscitation. You'd think, "It's just dead bones. There's no hope."

What God wants us to learn from this story is that nothing is too hard for Him. What may appear hopeless and dead to you and me is a field full of possibilities for the Lord.

Have you known people whom you thought were too far lost to be found—someone for whom it seemed useless to pray? The Bible says never give up!

When Mary asked, *"How can this be?"* the angel Gabriel told her, *"Nothing is impossible with God."* And when the disciples asked, *"Who then can be saved?"* Jesus answered, *"With men it is impossible, but not with God; for with God all things are possible."* The Bible is saying that without Christ, we can't do anything, but through Christ all things are possible. God never wants us to lose faith that He can give life—even if it appears that a situation is hopeless. We have all heard the proverb where there is life there is hope (Ecclesiastes 9:4). Yet with God, there is even hope when there appears to be no life!

WHEN GOD SPEAKS, THINGS HAPPEN

Next, God said to Ezekiel, *"Prophesy upon these bones, and say unto them, O ye dry bones, hear the word of the* LORD*"* (verse 4).

If you were to walk down the street one day and see a preacher standing on a box preaching to a skeleton, what would you think? You'd telephone the nearest mental hospital, wouldn't you? You'd assume that man was a menace to society.

Preaching to dry bones would seem like a waste of time. A skeleton just isn't listening! But we sometimes forget the incredible vital power of God's Word. If God can speak matter into existence with just a word and if He can make a man out of clay or a woman out of a rib, then it stands to reason that He can also cause the spiritually dead to hear. So don't lose hope, especially those of you who are pastors and evangelists! You can preach to dry bones and see results. God's Word is so potent and so powerful that it infuses new life into that which appears dead.

Whenever the Lord speaks, things happen. The Bible tells us that when Christ said to the leper, *"Be cleansed,"* he was immediately clean (Mark 1:40-42). When Jesus said, *"Get up and walk,"* to a man who had not walked in 38 years, the man walked (John 5:5-9). There is always inherent power in the Word of God to enable us to do whatever He commands.

LIFE IN THE BONES

In Ezekiel 37:5, God says, *"Behold, I will cause breath to enter into you, and ye shall live."*

Bones are almost always associated with death, yet Scripture tells one story in which bones were a source of life. In 2 Kings 13:20, 21, we find that Elisha the prophet, who was filled with a double portion of Elijah's spirit, was so Spirit-filled that his bones radiated life even after he was dead!

The Bible says that after Elisha died and was buried, some men in Israel were performing a funeral ceremony for one of their friends. As they were carrying his remains out to bury him, they caught a glimpse of Moabite raiders on horseback. These land pirates had been ransacking the countryside, and the Israelite men knew that they needed to get out of there fast or they'd be the next victims. They didn't want to be disrespectful toward the friend they were burying, but they had to run for their lives. So the Bible says that *"they cast the man into the sepulchre of Elisha: and when the man was let down, and touched the bones of Elisha, he revived, and stood up on his feet"* (verse 21).

There are also many modern-day examples of how bones can give life. In its June 1997 issue, Reader's Digest told about a family in which the daughter contracted a form of leukemia that would ultimately kill her unless she received a bone marrow transplant. Because she had an unusual blood type, it was very difficult to find a donor. So her parents did something that was almost unbelievable. They began praying to have another child with the same rare blood type. They hoped this second child, after a short time, would be able to provide the bone marrow needed for their daughter with leukemia.

Things were somewhat complicated by the fact that this was an older couple and the man had already had a vasectomy. Not only would doctors need to reverse that, which is a very iffy procedure in itself, but their new baby would need to have the same rare blood type as the older sister.

It worked. The man's surgery was a success, the couple was able to conceive again, and they gave birth to a second daughter who had the appropriate blood type. After 14 months, the little girl provided enough bone marrow, from her hip, to give a transplant that saved her older sister's life. There is life in the bones!

A MIGHTY, VAST ARMY

Ezekiel 37:7 says, *"So I prophesied as I was commanded: and as I prophesied, there was a noise, and behold a shaking, and the bones came together, bone to his bone."*

When God's people preach the truth, it's going to cause a rattling. Things are going to happen. Sometimes it brings revival. At other times it arouses opposition or persecution. Sometimes both! But I guarantee that when the truth is faithfully proclaimed, there's going to be a lot of shaking!

Imagine the prophet standing in this valley, ankle-deep in thousands of sun-bleached skeletons. After months of being ravaged by vultures and animals of carrion, this virtual sea of helter-skelter bones had been scattered all over the place. Then, as Ezekiel began to preach, there was a rattling. Suddenly as if drawn by some powerful unseen magnet, bones began to whiz and fly through the air, being pulled back to their original partners as God began the amazing process of reassembly.

After the bones came together in their appropriate positions and Ezekiel continued preaching, the Bible says that sinew and tendons began to take their places. Next the skin was put in position. Notice that God was doing things in order. He did not say, "Let's put all the flesh together. OK, now let's see if we can squeeze the bones inside the skin. Now let's put the muscle on the outside." That would have been backwards (and the result hideous). God always works through process and does things in their proper order—whether it is rebuilding His church or reviving us individually. *"Let all things be done decently and in order,"* the Bible says in 1 Corinthians 14:40.

Peter tells us that growing in Christ is also a process with order. *"Add to your faith virtue; and to virtue knowledge; And to knowledge temperance; and to temperance patience; and to patience godliness; And to godliness brotherly kindness; and to brotherly kindness charity"* (2 Peter 1:5–7).

At this point all the body parts were in their proper place. The bones, muscle and skin were in position, but still there was no life. The brain was in the head, but it wasn't thinking. The lungs were there, but the body wasn't breathing. The heart was in place, but it was not beating. Like Adam before the Lord inflated him with the breath of life, each soldier was a perfect lifeless corpse.

So now Ezekiel is surrounded not with thousands of disconnected bones, but with an army of cold bodies. They were probably very good-looking corpses, but they were dead nonetheless. This condition accurately describes some churches. They might have everything in place, but there is no spiritual life. Jesus says of them: *"I know thy works, that thou hast a name that thou livest, and art dead"* (Revelation 3:1). Outwardly, the members look really good. They think they're rich and increased with goods and in need of nothing (Revelation 3:17), yet they do not have the breath of life.

Ezekiel 37:10 says, *"So I prophesied as he commanded me, and the breath came into them, and they lived, and stood up upon their feet, an exceeding great army."*

God gives them life to fight. They become an army. In the same way, God gives us spiritual life so we can become soldiers in His army. We come to the Lord, He breathes into us the breath of life, then we go for the Lord. Zechariah 4:6 describes the battle plan: *"Not by might, nor by power, but by my spirit, saith the LORD of hosts."*

Hope for the Hopeless

After World War II, tens of thousands of Japanese soldiers and civilians were killed in Saipan. And today, 55 years later, teams of volunteers are still combing the region, searching for the bones of individuals who disappeared. It's very important for the survivors to be able to identify their missing relatives. Thus far they have found less than half of the people. That would be a very depressing job, don't you think? How much better to be involved in bringing life to bones that really can live—to people who can experience new life by virtue of the Word of God and the Spirit of God.

In verse 11, God says to Ezekiel, *"Son of man, these bones are the whole house of Israel: behold, they say, Our bones are dried, and our hope is lost: we are cut off for our parts."*

Have you ever felt cut off, dried up, or even hopeless?

Ezekiel 37:1–14 is a vision of hope. It's a wonderful message that God's Word and His Spirit can bring life to any situation and to any soul—no matter how utterly dead and hopeless it might be. Perhaps you remember the story where the dry, dead rod of Aaron came to life. After being placed in the ark of God overnight, it budded, flowered, and produced almonds (Numbers 17:8)! If God can make an old stick fruitful in His presence, He can do the same for us.

As a church, God can revive us and make us an army that will be part of His end-time remnant. Ezekiel 37:12–14 tells us that God's people will be raised up and brought into the Promised Land. There will be a resurrection of the righteous someday soon, and we will ultimately live in that new earth in the New Jerusalem. But even before that, the Lord wants to raise up an army of Spirit-filled people who will expand His kingdom.

Some of us do a pretty good job of covering up our dry bones. Maybe our marriages are dry and barren. Or maybe there has been a loss of vitality in our family or work relationships. Some of us have bank accounts that are like dry bones. Others have health problems. Whatever the cause, the message in this study is that God can send new life to your dry bone situation. God can breathe vitality through His Spirit and through His Word into our lives. Pray for that revival today.

The Secret Weapon
Chapter Thirteen

" **F**or the word of God is quick, and powerful, and sharper than any two-edged sword, piercing even to the dividing asunder of soul and spirit, and of the joints and marrow, and is a discerner of the thoughts and intents of the heart" (Hebrews 4:12).

I could hear the sound of his three-wheel bicycle squeak up behind me as I walked down the street. Brother Harold was a living legend among the young people in Palm Springs. He was a 70-year-old saint who knew how to "walk the walk" and "talk the talk." His day began at 4 a.m. with two hours of Bible study and prayer, followed by a few hours on the street handing out tracts. Next he was off to the hospital. As a self-appointed chaplain, he would visit the rooms and share an encouraging scripture or two with the patients—all from memory. I will never forget how his voice quivered with reverence when he quoted the Bible. One time at an early-morning prayer meeting, I thought I saw his old bearded face shine as he prayed.

I was a new convert about 17 years old, still struggling to separate my former hippie philosophy from the truths of the Bible. Needless to say, I was feeling a bit like a failure as a Christian.

"What a glorious day God has given us!" Brother Harold called as he pulled up beside me with his oversized tricycle. He was always so up.

"Yeah, nice day," I responded. I must not have been very convincing, because he detected from my voice that something was missing. He studied me for a moment with a loving yet concerned expression.

"How long can you hold your breath, Doug?" Brother Harold suddenly asked with a twinkle in his eye. His question surprised me, but I seldom missed an opportunity to brag. In school I had played a little game of seeing how long I could hold my breath while waiting for the class bell to ring.

I boasted, "I can hold my breath for 4 minutes, if I hyperventilate first."

"Then you should not go any longer than that without praying," Brother Harold quipped. "God's Word tells us, 'Pray without ceasing.'" Next he asked, "How often do you eat?"

Now I was beginning to sense where he was leading. "About two or three times a day," I slowly answered.

"Well that's how often you should read or meditate on God's Word," he said. Then he added, "Doug, what will happen to your body if you never exercise it?"

"I suppose I'll get weak and flabby," I responded.

"That's right," said Brother Harold, "and that is what will happen to your faith if you don't use it and share it."

As he peddled away, Brother Harold called over his shoulder, "The same laws that apply to your physical body also apply to your spiritual health."

That day, 20 years ago in Palm Springs, Brother Harold directed me to the secret weapon for the Christian. That weapon is our personal devotions—Bible study, prayer, and witnessing. It's not a secret weapon because it is a hidden truth, but rather a neglected truth.

George Mueller said this about God's Word: "The vigor of our spiritual life will be in exact proportion to the place held by the Bible in our life and thoughts."

Salvation leans very heavily on the necessity of knowing God. *"And this is life eternal, that they might know thee, the only true God, and Jesus Christ, whom thou hast sent"* (John 17:3).

Remember that Jesus said, speaking of the lost, *"And then will I profess unto them, I never knew you: depart from me, ye that work iniquity"* (Matthew 7:23). And in Hosea 4:6, God declares, *"My people are destroyed for lack of knowledge."*

This knowledge that saves is not a casual understanding of biblical doctrine. The devil has that, but it will not save him. James 2:19, *"the devils also believe, and tremble."*

To know God means to have a loving relationship with Him. *"I will even betroth thee unto me in faithfulness: and thou shalt know the* LORD*"* (Hosea 2:20).

We can't really obey the Lord unless we love Him first. This is why Jesus said, *"If you love Me, keep My commandments"* (John 14:15).

We all know how important it is for a Christian to have faith. Where do we get faith? Paul tells us, *"So then faith cometh by hearing, and hearing by the word of God"* (Romans 10:17).

It is a very simple formula.

To obey God, we must love Him. To love God, we must know Him.

To know or trust anybody, we must first take time to communicate with them. They talk to us, and we to them.

God speaks to us through His Word, and we speak to Him through prayer. The more we know God, the better we will love Him. The better we love Him, the better we will serve Him.

Morning is the best time for getting to know God. This principle was deeply impressed upon the children of Israel through His gift of manna. It rained down from heaven early in the morning, six days a week. If they waited too long, the manna would evaporate. *"And they gathered it every morning, every man according to his eating: and when the sun waxed hot, it melted"* (Exodus 16:21).

If we wait too long to have our devotions, the cares and pressures of the day will get our attention before the Lord does. Let's not let the manna melt! Remember, the busier we are and the more we have to do, the more we need to take time to pray.

Having morning devotions was also the practice of Jesus, our perfect example. *"And in the morning, rising up a great while before day, he went out, and departed into a solitary place, and there prayed"* (Mark 1:35).

It is important that we consider eating spiritual food just as essential as physical food. If we are late for work and must choose between our raisin bran or personal devotions, most people feel that our quiet time with God is expendable. Fiber is important, but it will not keep you from sin that day.

Job 23:12 says, *"I have esteemed the words of his mouth more than my necessary food."*

When we pray, *"Give us this day our daily bread,"* it should apply more to the spiritual bread than the baked variety (Matthew 6:11). When Jesus was tempted in the wilderness after a 40-day fast, He told the devil, *"It is written, That man shall not live by bread alone, but by every word of God"* (Luke 4:4).

I can't explain it, but it seems that spiritual food gave Jesus not just spiritual strength, but also physical strength. John 4:31, 32 says, *"In the mean while, his disciples prayed him, saying, Master, eat. But he said unto them, I have meat to eat that ye know not of."*

Elijah received supernatural physical strength from eating

heavenly bread an angel prepared. *"And the angel of the LORD came again the second time, and touched him, and said, Arise and eat; because the journey is too great for thee. And he arose, and did eat and drink, and went in the strength of that meat forty days and forty nights unto Horeb the mount of God"* (1 Kings 19:7, 8).

You may even find that if you wake up a little earlier for more devotional time with God, you will have increased energy throughout the day.

If we want to be able to resist the daily temptations that assail us, we need the same secret weapon Jesus used. It is described in Ephesians 6:17: *"And take ... the sword of the Spirit, which is the word of God."*

We all desperately need and want to have Jesus abiding in our hearts; how do we get Him there? Another name for Jesus is "The Word." In reading the Word, we are directly inviting Jesus into our hearts and minds. *"Thy word have I hid in mine heart, that I might not sin against thee"* (Psalm 119:11).

Since Jesus is the Word, it would also be safe to say that Jesus Himself is the secret weapon! The principle is that as we spend more time with Jesus through prayer and Bible study, we will know Him better, and therefore love Him better. Just as our natural reaction is to talk about those we love, so it will become more natural for us to tell others about our Lord. Then, as we share our faith with others, our own faith will become stronger—just as a muscle is strengthened by activity.

More love, more witnessing, better surrender, more energy, less depression—all this and much more is a direct chain reaction that comes from using the secret weapon of personal devotions.

So how long can you hold your breath?

WHAT SHALL I WEAR?
CHAPTER FOURTEEN

An Amazing Fact: In the extreme temperatures and near vacuum of interplanetary space, astronauts need special clothing to survive. Their spacesuits supply them with oxygen, regulate their body temperatures, remove moisture, and monitor blood pressure and heart rate.

When Neil Armstrong went on the Apollo 11 mission that made him the first man to land on the moon, his suit was specifically designed to provide a life-sustaining environment during periods of extra-vehicular activity or un-pressurized spacecraft operation. The custom-fitted spacesuit permitted maximum mobility and was designed to be worn with relative comfort for up to 115 hours outside the spacecraft or for 14 days in an un-pressurized mode.

Astronauts must put an enormous amount of trust in their spacesuits. One space-adventurer admitted it was eerie to know that while outside the space capsule, there was just one-quarter of an inch between him and eternity. Now that's important clothing!

Man is different from every other creature in regard to clothing. All of the other creatures in God's kingdom were "born with their clothes on," so to speak. The covering they need grows from the inside out, and some animals even shed their old clothes periodically and develop new ones. Man is the only creature whose clothes must come from the outside.

The Bible tells us that artificial clothing was first introduced after Adam and Eve ate the forbidden fruit in Eden. Genesis 3:7 says, *"The eyes of them both were opened, and they knew that they were naked; and they sewed fig leaves together, and made themselves aprons."*

The Hebrew word for "aprons" is the equivalent of "belts." In an attempt to cover their nakedness, using their own resourcefulness, they sewed themselves belts of fig leaves. Until that time, Adam and Eve had never witnessed death, so they probably thought the leaves would work just fine as a permanent cover-up for their shame. However, when the fig leaves began to shrivel, Adam and Eve discovered that their homespun remedy wasn't going to work.

God had to tell the wayward couple that their skimpy fig belts were not appropriate. He also explained that the sacrifice of another creature would be required for them to be properly clothed.

The Bible says, *"Also for Adam and his wife the LORD God made tunics of skin, and clothed them"* (Genesis 3:21, NKJV). The phrase "tunics of skin" literally means "robes of skin." Man fashioned miniskirts, but God made robes instead.

WHY DO WE WEAR CLOTHES?

This brings us to the first reason we wear clothes: modesty. The principle foundation why God distributed clothing was to cover Adam' and Eve's nakedness. Consequently, when those of us who are Christians come to worship the Lord, we need to be sure that everything we wear is high enough, low enough, and loose enough to cover our bodies because we are in the presence of a holy God. In Isaiah 6:2–3, we find that even the angels around the throne of God, who minister in His presence, veil their faces and their feet and cry, *"Holy, holy, holy."*

In addition to modesty, another reason we wear clothing is to protect us from harsh temperatures and climates. In certain parts of the world, clothing must keep us warm, while in other parts it must keep us cool and protect us from too much sun or wind.

There's a very touching story in the last letter Paul wrote before he was executed. Paul was in prison, and he knew that his remaining days were few. He said: *"I am now ready to be offered, and the time of my departure is at hand. I have fought a good fight, I have finished my course, I have kept the faith"* (2 Timothy 4:6-7).

At the end of the letter, Paul includes several special requests directed to his dear friend Timothy. He asks, *"Bring the cloak that I left with Carpus at Troas when you come—and the books, especially the parchments"* (verse 13, NKJV).

Back then, prisons didn't have air conditioning or heat, and the only luxuries a prisoner might enjoy had to be supplied by his friends or family. Paul was getting old, and he was cold. I can empathize with the aged apostle when he says, *"Please bring my cloak that I left, and come quickly—before winter"* (verses 13, 9, 21). For me, it's easier to endure heat than cold, so I'm thankful that God gave us clothing to protect us from the elements.

Another reason we wear clothing is to show respect. What we wear says something about what we are doing, where we are going, and whom we are planning to see.

Different clothing is appropriate for different occasions. For instance, you wouldn't wear the same outfit to go out picnicking with your family as you would to go to work at a fast-food restaurant. Likewise, when you come to worship before the Lord, you would not wear the same clothes that you'd wear if going to the beach.

This is something that I believe is very important. Those of us on the church staff where I pastor usually do a lot of cleaning and yard work at the church on Fridays to get ready for Sabbath, so we don't wear our suits. Friday is our casual day.

Not too long ago, I went to the church on a Friday wearing jeans, a sweatshirt, tennis shoes, and a baseball cap. There was so much to do that I didn't have time to go home and change before the prophecy Bible study that evening. Fortunately my associate pastor was teaching. However, I had to help him set up the projector and the computer beforehand. About the time that I finished, people were starting to arrive for the study and I was embarrassed because I had a day-and-a-half's worth of beard—which on me doesn't look very good. So I snuck out around the side of the building and went into the youth room to listen. I just did not feel right about being in a sacred place for a formal gathering looking like that.

Some of you might say, "It doesn't matter what we wear to church, because God looks on your heart."

Wrong. For me, it does matter because I know better, and I think it would be a bad witness if I came into the house of the Lord looking grubby when we're studying God's Word. Out of respect for God, I don't feel comfortable doing that.

Sometimes people come to church looking like they're going to the beach or on some other casual outing. Now if those are the best clothes they own, then God will certainly bless and they should come anyway. But if they have better clothes hanging in their closet, they need to choose those to wear to church.

Let's face it: Most people, if invited to the governor's house for dinner, wouldn't wear blue jeans or beach clothes. How sad to show more respect for a politician, a mere earthly ruler, than for the King of the universe! If we give our best to sinful mortals and show more regard for men than we do for our Creator and Redeemer, then we have misplaced our priorities. When we come before the Lord, we should wear our best—whatever it happens to be.

Another reason we wear clothing is identification. For example, it is important at times to be able to recognize a police officer. When an officer is undercover and working without a uniform, you can't spot him or her in a crowd. If you were in trouble, you would have to rely on them noticing you because you wouldn't know that help was nearby.

During the Gulf War, it was important for U.S. soldiers to wear uniforms identifying them as Americans so that they wouldn't accidentally be killed from friendly fire.

My parents sent me to military school when I was 5 years old, and we had three different kinds of uniforms. One was for class, one was for parades, and another was for dirty work. I actually liked it because I never had to wonder what to wear. They told us every single day.

Many schools are currently debating whether or not it is best to require students to wear uniforms. I feel that uniforms are better. I went to 14 different schools when I was a kid—public schools, private schools and Catholic schools. Some had uniforms, and some did not. I found that the students at schools where uniforms were required typically were not as preoccupied with who was better than whom. They could focus more on relationships and schoolwork than on making a fashion statement of who was rich and who was poor.

Clothing was used as identification in Bible times, as well. For example, Jacob gave Joseph a multicolored robe (Genesis 37:3), which was an ancient symbol for royalty that was given only to very special children. King David's daughters also wore coats of many colors (2 Samuel 13:18). In another story, the crafty Gibeonites tricked the Israelites into believing they were ambassadors from a distant country by wearing old tattered clothes, patched sandals, and by carrying moldy bread and worn-out canteens (Joshua 9:3–16). In the New Testament, we find that John the Baptist stood out in the crowd because he wore simple, modest clothing in a day when the political and religious leaders loved to wear ornaments and long, flowing robes. Mark 1:6 says that he wore a robe of camel hair and a belt of skin around his waist. It's no wonder that the Jews who saw John were reminded of the prophet Elijah, who also wore a garment of hair and was girded with a leather belt (2 Kings 1:8). Last but not least, two women are mentioned in Revelation 12 and 17. One woman represents God's church, while the other represents an apostate, or fallen, church. These women never speak. Not once in the Bible do they open their mouths to utter a word. Yet we can identify who they are because the Bible tells us what they are wearing (Revelation 12:1; 17:4–5) and what they are doing (Revelation 12:2, 5–6; 17:1–3, 6).

The fact that clothing is used as identification leads us to a very important point. It is said that you shouldn't judge a book by its cover, but most people do. If a publisher wants a book to sell well, then it better have a good cover. Even though it may not be fair, that's the way it works. Likewise, people should not necessarily judge others by the clothes they are wearing, but they do. So as a Christian, you don't want to wear anything that might give someone the wrong impression of whose servant you are.

So What Shall We Wear?

The Bible mentions several things we should remember to wear. One thing that everybody should put on is a smile. Now you're probably thinking, "That's really cute, but it's not biblical."

Actually, it is biblical. Job 9:27 (NKJV) says, *"I will put off my sad face and wear a smile."* So the first thing we want to put on is a cheerful countenance. Many of us could do a lot more to advertise for Jesus simply by being happier. Too many Christians go around looking like they've been baptized in lemon juice, then they wonder why their friends and family aren't interested in hearing their testimony. I believe that many more individuals would want to be Christians if we would look more positive and happy about our relationship with Jesus.

In addition to a smile, we need to put on the armor of God. Ephesians 6:11 says, *"Put on the whole armour of God, that ye may be able to stand against the wiles of the devil."* God supplies it for us, but you and I must make time to put it on each day.

Have you read Hans Christian Anderson's fairy tale entitled *The*

Emperor's New Clothes? In this story, two scoundrels take advantage of their vain emperor by claiming that they have invented a method to weave a cloth so light and fine that it looks invisible to all who are too stupid and incompetent to appreciate its quality. They supposedly present the emperor with a garment made of this cloth, which of course he can't see. However, not wanting to look ignorant, he pretends to admire its fine workmanship and beautiful colors. The scoundrels encourage the emperor to take a ride through the city to show off his beautiful new "garment." He does so, and the people praise and compliment him because they don't want to look like fools either. A little boy finally points out the obvious: the emperor is naked!

When we talk about the armor of God, we are not simply describing imaginary clothes. The Bible says that we are to wear the helmet of salvation, the breastplate of righteousness, the sword of the Spirit, the belt of truth, and the gospel shoes (Ephesians 6:14–17). These are real, tangible things that we must put on each day. We do this, for example, by putting the Word of God in our hearts and our minds and by taking it wherever we go. These various implements really do work. They are exactly what Jesus used to combat the devil in the wilderness of temptation (Luke 4:1–13), and they are available for us every day.

If we're going to be effective in saving others, we need to be properly clad. Romans 13:12 tells us: *"The night is far spent, the day is at hand: let us therefore cast off the works of darkness, and let us put on the armour of light."* Jesus said that people ought to look at us and see that we've got a light. *"Let your light so shine before men, that they may see your good works, and glorify your Father which is in heaven"* (Matthew 5:16).

I like the story in the Old Testament where Jonathan—Saul's son, the crown prince—took off his armor, robe, sword and belt and gave them to David (1 Samuel 18:4). Many of you know that Karen and I named our youngest son Nathan, which means "gift." Jonathan means "Jehovah's gift." Isn't it interesting that Jehovah's gift gave David his armor, his robe, his sword and his spear? Jesus gives us these same things too. He provides His armor for us.

DO OUR CLOTHES MATTER?

In Matthew 22, we find a parable Jesus told about the king who planned a wedding feast and invited all of his servants to come.

At most low-budget weddings today, the bridesmaids buy their own dresses and the groomsmen rent their own tuxedos. However, at some of the more lavish weddings, the couple's sponsors will buy all of the dresses and pay for the tuxedos. When the king has a wedding for his son, you can be sure that he will supply the necessary garments. That was automatically understood in this parable, especially when you consider that the king had to go out in the highways and the byways and the hedges to get people to come to the wedding banquet. Those poor people certainly didn't have appropriate wedding garments. The king provided the clothing at his own expense.

However, incredibly the Bible tells us that someone showed up without the wedding garment. When asked how he could have been so careless, the man was speechless (verse 12). He had no excuse. The king had purchased a garment for him; he simply didn't take the time or energy to don the garment that had been provided. Consequently, the king said to his servants: *"Bind him hand and foot, and take him away, and cast him into outer darkness; there shall be weeping and gnashing of teeth"* (verse 13).

This parable is especially relevant for us today, because it's important to be wearing the right type of clothing when Jesus comes. Scripture tells us that the Lord is coming soon for His special bride. *"As Christ also loved the church, and gave himself for it; That he might sanctify and cleanse it with the washing of water by the word, That he might present it to himself a glorious church, not having spot, or wrinkle, or any such thing; but that it should be holy and without blemish"* (Ephesians 5:25–27).

You might be thinking, "How do I get garments that are without spot or without wrinkle?" In Revelation 3:18, Jesus says, *"I counsel thee to buy of me gold tried in the fire, that thou mayest be rich; and white raiment, that thou mayest be clothed, and that the shame of thy nakedness do not appear."* Our pure white garments come from Jesus. He does not charge a high price for them; salvation is a free gift (Romans 6:23). The Lord wants nothing but the gold of our faith and the silver of our love. That is the currency we use to secure this fine new clothing.

The next question you might have is: "Once I get the spotless white garment, how do I keep it clean?"

Revelation 7:14 gives us the answer. Our garments are washed in the blood of the Lamb. When you come to Jesus, He gives you a spotless white robe. This is justification, which means that you come to the Lord just as you are and He covers you with His perfect robe of righteousness. What follows is sanctification, a process in which you learn how to keep that robe clean, during which the blood of the Lamb cleanses your very nature. His blood is readily available, but it is infinitely precious so we don't want to carelessly soil the pure robes He gives us.

TAKE ACTION!

Many of us have had easy access to a washer and dryer our entire lives, but others have not. One thing I've discovered is that when you have a washer and dryer right at hand, you're not as particular about keeping your clothes clean. One time when the washer and dryer broke at our cabin in the hills, I found myself wearing the same thing for several days because I didn't want to go to the trouble of washing them by hand. I also began to be a little more careful to keep my clothes clean since I knew that we didn't have a washer and dryer available.

I believe the Lord is now trying to teach us how to keep the spotless clothes He gives us forever clean. Many of us are waiting for some sort of special prescription to be handed out in the future that will teach us how to live victorious lives, but it has actually already been given to us.

Today, the grace of Jesus is constantly available to wash our sins away when we ask Him. However, we too often forget that it won't always be that way. A day is coming when Christ will proclaim that the "Laundromat" is closed. *"He which is filthy, let him be filthy still: and he that is righteous, let him be righteous still"* (Revelation 22:11).

Perhaps, like me, you're filled with amazement at God's generosity and can't comprehend how a life that has been so scarred and filthy can be suddenly washed and clothed in pure white. Remember that with God, all things are possible (Matthew 19:26).

Notice how the Bible says, *"Put on the armor"* and *"Buy from me white garments"* and *"Put on Christ."* God is inviting us to take action—to wear these things He has provided. In so doing, we will be putting on the characteristics of Christ that will serve as a powerful witness to others of the love and graciousness of God.

WHO WILL BE LEFT STANDING?
CHAPTER FIFTEEN

An Amazing Fact: Ancient Roman coliseums hosted brutal blood sports in which slaves, trained to be fierce fighters called gladiators, would battle one another to the death. Julius Caesar ordered large-scale exhibitions with 300 pairs of combatants on one occasion. But the largest contest of gladiators was given by the emperor Trajan as part of a victory celebration in A.D. 107. It featured a staggering 5,000 pairs of fighters! And sometimes, to provide spectators a little more "entertainment thrill," hungry, wild animals were released into the mix. The gladiators would then have to battle one another and the fanged creatures. Despite near-impossible odds, these slaves fought fiercely because they had a glimmer of hope: If they could survive the assaults of their fellow gladiators and wild animals, the emperor just might release them. The goal was simply to be the one left standing.

A CONSISTENT THEME

Who is going to be left standing? What is going to truly last?

The Bible clearly says that, in the last days, only a few will be left standing. Revelation 6:17 poses this important question: *"For the great day of his wrath is come; and who shall be able to stand?"* And Malachi 3:2 affirms: *"But who can endure the day of His coming? And who can stand when He appears? For He is like a refiner's fire* [and] *like fuller's soap"* (NKJV, emphasis added).

The Bible tells us that a great judgment day is coming. The last chapter in Daniel begins with Michael standing up, and after a great time of trouble it concludes with Daniel standing. *"Thou shalt rest, and stand in thy lot at the end of the days"* (Daniel 12:13).

The screens of our minds are burned with that picture of

Shadrach, Meshach and Abed-nego threatened with a fiery furnace. Yet they stood tall as the rest of the world bowed down to Nebuchadnezzar's image. They stood for Jehovah when everyone else fell.

Revelation 13 warns us of a coming storm similar to the one they faced—a day of reckoning. Most will bow down, but some will be left standing.

FAME AND FORTUNE WILL FALL

We often call it "Custer's Last Stand," but we should really say "Custer's Last Fall," because he didn't stand. It was the Indians' last stand, for standing means you're victorious—that you survived and are still around.

So maybe we should apply the process of elimination and learn what isn't going to stand or endure to the end. I think most of us already realize that some things people build on make pretty shabby foundations. Money is one of them—it's not going to last. Proverbs 11:4 says, *"Riches profit not in the day of wrath: but righteousness delivereth from death."* You will not be able to bribe the Judge when Jesus comes.

Proverbs 11:28 adds, *"He that trusteth in his riches shall fall: but the righteous shall flourish as a branch."* And then there is Isaiah 2:20, 21, speaking of the day of judgment, *"In that day a man shall cast his idols of silver, and his idols of gold, which they made each one for himself to worship, to the moles and to the bats ... for fear of the Lord, and for the glory of his majesty, when he ariseth to shake terribly the earth."* Money is not going to last.

How about fame? The Bible is very clear. *"The memory of the just is blessed: but the name of the wicked shall rot"* (Proverbs 10:7). *"The face of the Lord is against them that do evil, to cut off the remembrance of them from the earth"* (Psalm 34:16). And Daniel 12 tells us that the names of the wicked are covered with everlasting contempt. Instead of fame, they'll have infamy or obscurity.

WATER OF LIFE IS THICKER THAN BLOOD

Can we always count on our friends and family standing by us to the end? Sadly, we can't. Job 19:14 says, *"My kinsfolk have failed, and my familiar friends have forgotten me."* And Jesus adds, *"A man's foes shall be they of his own household"* (Matthew 10:36). Have you ever considered how many stories in the Bible are of a man's adversaries being his own relatives? Cain killed his brother. Who betrayed Joseph? His brothers. And Jesus? His own disciple, and His own people, handed Him over to the Romans. And in the last days, we'll probably see a repeat performance of that familial betrayal.

I sometimes get exasperated because some Christians still believe that in the last days we need to fear pagan religions, the New Age movement and such. But I'm not nearly as concerned about the obvious enemies on the outside as the ones on the inside. Prophecy tells us whom we need to watch; it's going to be those who share a common faith with us: the neighbors, our friends, our families. In the end, our neighbors will be our enemies. I've always wondered why Christ said to love your neighbors and then again love your enemies; could it be because they are often one and the same?

FAILING FOUNDATIONS

One would think that we could certainly trust the earth, right? It's pretty big; the solid ground we're standing on must be dependable. But the Bible says, *"The earth shall reel to and fro like a drunkard, and shall be removed like a cottage"* (Isaiah 24:20). Have you been in an earthquake? I've experienced a few while living in California. The ground trembles and rolls under your feet as if you were standing on a waterbed. It's very disconcerting, but it helps you realize there's very little in the world you can count on, including the very earth on which you stand. Matthew 24:35 warns, *"Heaven and earth shall pass away."* And 1 John 2:17 adds, *"And the world passeth away, and the lust thereof: but he that doeth the will of God abideth for ever."*

Samson's Fight

So what does it take to stand? First of all, you need to be filled with the Spirit. We have a story that vividly illustrates this in the book of Judges. In chapter 15:14, it says, *"And when [Samson] came unto Lehi, the Philistines shouted against him: and the spirit of the LORD came mightily upon him, and the cords that were upon his arms became as flax that was burnt with fire, and his bands loosed from off his hands."* The Philistines went to Israel with a price on Samson's head. So the fearful Israelites took Samson captive, tied him up, and abandoned him in a valley called Lehi. (Yet another case of family betrayal.) When the Philistines saw Samson bound and apparently defenseless, they surrounded him and shouted victory. But the Spirit of the Lord came upon Samson, and he snapped the ropes like thread.

He reached down and picked up a donkey jawbone, and the Bible says he commenced fighting against the continuous wave of armed forces seeking to arrest him. There were 1,000 soldiers—a ratio of 1,000 to one! And the one won. *"And Samson said, With the jawbone of [a donkey], heaps upon heaps"* (verse 16). What do you think the scene looked like when Samson was done with that battle? He was surrounded with piles of slain Philistines. He was the only one left standing.

"A thousand shall fall at thy side, and ten thousand at thy right hand; but it shall not come nigh thee. Only with thine eyes shalt thou behold and see the reward of the wicked" (Psalm 91:7, 8).

This event was also a fulfillment of a prophecy. In Joshua 23:10, the Bible says, *"One man of you shall chase a thousand: for the LORD your God, he it is that fighteth for you, as he hath promised you."*

How did Samson remain standing? Notice it was after he was filled with the Spirit and his bonds were burst, which is a symbol for us. If we remain bound with sin, the enemy can easily torment and overcome us (Jeremiah 30:8). However, if we are liberated by Jesus and filled with His power, we are invincible!

An Empty Sack

It's hard to make an empty sack stand up, but when you fill it, it will stand much more easily. It's the same principle with us. If you want to stand in the last days, you can't be an empty sack. We must be filled with God's Spirit.

The Bible tells us of a powerful threefold confederacy that will oppose God's people in the last days. The saints will be greatly outnumbered. Yet they will stand. Remember that when the Egyptians came against Israel, God's people asked, *"What are we going to do?"* God answered them, *"Stand still. I'll fight for you"* (Exodus 14:13). And in 2 Chronicles 20:17, 21–24, a confederacy of evil nations arises to annihilate Judah and Israel. It looked impossible to Judah's king, Jehoshaphat. His army was greatly outnumbered. (It is again interesting to note that the confederacy was made up of the Edomites, Moabites and Ammonites—nations related to Israel; i.e., family.)

This axis power surrounded Judah on three sides. It looked hopeless, until God spoke through a prophet. He said to the king, *"Ye shall not need to fight in this battle: set yourselves, stand ye still, and see the salvation of the LORD with you."* And do you know what the king did next? *"And when he had consulted with the people, he appointed singers unto the LORD, and that should praise the beauty of holiness."* Would you go into battle choosing the choir as your first wave of attack? Yet that's exactly what Israel did. *"They went out before the army, and [said], Praise the LORD; for his mercy endureth for ever."* And when they began to sing and to praise the Lord, their enemies *"...were smitten. For the children of Ammon and Moab stood up against the inhabitants of Mount Seir, utterly to slay and destroy them: and when they had made an end of the [Edomites], the inhabitants of mount Seir, every one helped to destroy another. And when Judah came toward the watch tower in the wilderness, they looked unto the multitude, and, behold, they were dead bodies fallen to the earth, and none escaped."*

Three entire nations stood against the armies of Israel, and they self-destructed. They became suspicious and turned on one another. They became confused, as everybody's sword was against his comrade, until the last two stabbed each other simultaneously and fell over dead. No enemies were left standing. Only the children of Israel were standing after the battle. All they had left to do was collect the spoils of war.

LAST-DAY STAND

So how do we prepare to stand? Well, first we've got to ensure that we're wearing the whole armor of God. Open your Bible to Psalm 91—a beautiful, extraordinary promise for those who don this armor to stand in the last days. The Lord says that for those who abide and trust in Him, *"under the shadow of the Almighty,"* will be spared from the "snare of the fowler"—that's the devil trying to trap us. Not only will we stand with Him, we also won't be afraid, for His truth will be our *"shield and buckler."*

And don't miss again, *"A thousand shall fall at thy side,"* like Samson, *"and ten thousand at thy right hand."* Just picture that if you will. A thousand at your side and 10,000 at your right hand—all fallen; yet you're standing taller than ever before.

But how is it that so many could fall, yet you be left standing? Psalm 91 continues, *"But it shall not come nigh thee. Only with thine eyes shalt thou behold and see the reward of the wicked. Because thou hast made the LORD, which is my refuge, even the most High, thy habitation; There shall no evil befall thee, neither shall any plague come nigh thy dwelling."* During the seven last plagues, God will protect those who are faithful to Him, who abide in Him. And how will He do this? *"For he shall give his angels charge over thee, to keep thee in all thy ways."* Angels do more than protect us from physical harm. In fact, I believe God principally sends them to keep us in His will and way. *"Thou shalt tread upon the lion and adder: the young lion and the dragon shalt thou trample under feet."* The lion and serpent here are symbols of the devil, a roaring lion (1 Peter 5:8).

This means that you will stand upon a fallen devil. He's below you when you have God's protection. When temptations come, by the grace of God, you can be victorious.

STANDING WITH LOVE, FAITH AND GRACE

However, one important prerequisite for standing and deliverance promised in Psalm 91 is often missed. *"Because he hath set his love upon me, therefore will I deliver him."* In this case, love isn't something that just comes spontaneously, like a sudden weather change. Here, love is a choice. And if you make this choice to set your love upon Him, notice what happens: *"He shall call upon me, and I will answer him: I will be with him in trouble; I will deliver him, and honour him. With long life will I satisfy him, and shew him my salvation."*

And then we read, *"Let all that you do be done with love."* Why with love? Because, as 1 Corinthians 13:8 explains, *"Love never fails."*

Let's continue with Psalm 91. What is another important factor for standing in the last days? *"I will set him on high, because he hath known my name."* We need to know God. Remember, Jesus declares to the lost, *"I don't know you."* But even more, it says we need to know His name. There is power in the name of the Lord. Do you utilize that power? Do you pray in His name?

"For by faith ye stand" (2 Corinthians 1:24). How do we stand in the last days? By works? No, because anybody who defeats 1,000 people has something more then physical prowess. They need faith! And 1 Corinthians 16:13 adds, *"Watch ye, stand fast in the faith, quit you like men, be strong."*

And 1 Peter 5:12 tells us, *"This is the true grace of God wherein ye stand."* We will never fall if we know the Lord and stand in faith, love, and grace.

STANDING FOR THE WORD

Those who know the Word of God will be left standing. And with this, another unusual Bible battle comes to mind. The Bible speaks of the mighty men of David. In 1 Chronicles 11, it tells about one of the these mighty men named Eleazar and his king David. *"There the Philistines were gathered together to battle ... and the people fled from before the Philistines. And [Eleazar and David] set themselves in the midst [of a barley field] ... and slew the Philistines; and the LORD saved them by a great deliverance"* (vs. 13, 14). In 2 Samuel 23:10, it says of Eleazar, *"His hand was weary, and his hand clave unto the sword: and the LORD wrought a great victory that day."*

Eleazar and David remained, standing back to back, defeating all their attackers, even after their countrymen left. They would not retreat. They took a stand when everyone else fell. And just like Samson, they were left standing. They could only do that because they knew and trusted in God, and the Lord gave them victory.

We are living in a day when many of God's people are cowering and fleeing before the enemy. They are ridiculed for taking the Word of God too literally. You are considered a zealot if you believe you should follow Christ and keep the commandments.

So you may find a day soon when you stand alone. Will you still stand through the persecutions to come? The word "standards" comes from "stand"—it means you stand for something. And I've got news for you, friend: As we approach the last days, if you don't stand for something, you're going to fall for anything. You'll retreat.

Did you also catch that David and Eleazar took their stand in the midst of a barley field? What is grain a symbol of in the Bible? The Word of God is our bread from heaven. They put their lives on the line to defend a field of grain. They clung to their swords, which are also symbols for God's Word—which is actually sharper and quicker than any double-edged sword (Hebrews 4:12). And in Revelation, Christ is seen with a two-edged sword coming out of His mouth. The edges represent the two witnesses: the New and the Old Testaments. And because Eleazar and David clung to the Word, God fought for them and they were victorious. The same promises belong to us, if we cling to and defend the Word.

Ephesians 6 says that the secret to standing is being armed for spiritual battles with spiritual equipment. *"Put on the whole amour of God, that ye may be able to stand against the wiles of the devil ... that ye may be able to withstand in the evil day, and having done all, to stand. Stand therefore, having your loins girt about with truth ... and the sword of the Spirit, which is the word of God"* (vs. 11, 13, 14, 17).

"Heaven and earth shall pass away," but the Word of God will not pass away. And Isaiah 40:8 offers an even more solid picture: *"The grass withereth, the flower fadeth: but the word of our God shall stand for ever."*

What is dependable? God's Word; it is going to stand.

So if we stand up for God's Word, the truth—even though it's not popular—we'll be left standing. Some truth that's accepted today will become increasingly unpopular as time ends. You need to decide now if you're going to retreat with everybody else or if you're going to stand, fighting back to back with Jesus, the son of David. He will not ever leave you nor forsake you (Hebrews 13:5).

STANDING BEFORE THE SON

A wonderful story found in John 8 perfectly illustrates this picture. The religious leaders caught a woman in adultery, and they brought her before Jesus to receive the death decree. With self-righteous indignation, they stood pointing accusing fingers, ready and eager to snuff out her life under a hail of stones.

They pressed their question, "What do you say?" But He ignored them. Instead, He stooped down and began to sketch in the dust on the temple floor as though they were not there. Then He stood up next to the woman who was caught in adultery and said those immortalized words: *"He that is without sin among you, let him first cast a stone at her."*

And then Jesus knelt down again and waited. Ashamed and bewildered, the leaders pondered their next move. But soon, they began to see what Jesus was writing in the dust; they saw that He was writing out their very own sins.

After recognizing this, the accusers began crawling away one by one—like cockroaches shaken by the light. *"And they which heard it, being convicted by their own conscience, went out one by one, beginning at the eldest even unto the last: and Jesus was left alone, and the woman standing in the midst"* (John 8:9).

Her accusers were gone; they fell, but she was face to face with Jesus—standing.

WHO IS WORTHY TO STAND?

How could this woman, which many believe to be Mary Magdalene, stand under those circumstances? She broke the commandments. She was unworthy. But what does Christ say to her? *"Woman, where are those thine accusers? hath no man condemned thee?"* She answers, *"No man, Lord."* And Jesus replies, *"Neither do I condemn thee: go, and sin no more."*

Christ also said, *"Watch ye therefore, and pray always, that ye may be accounted worthy to escape all these things that shall come to pass, and to stand before the Son of man"* (Luke 21:36). Notice that Jesus doesn't say you will be worthy—He says that you will be counted worthy. Mary was guilty of sin, but did He count her guilty? No, He gave her mercy. She stood in grace because He would take her penalty.

Who is going to be left standing? The ones who love the Lord. The ones who have faith and stand in grace. The ones not afraid to stand alone with Jesus—they will be left standing. But you might be thinking, "I fall all the time. How can I know I'll stand in the end?" Well, Proverbs 24:16 says, *"For a just man falleth seven times, and riseth up again."* Jesus cast seven demons from Mary; she fell into her old patterns several times. But as often as she sincerely repented of it, He genuinely forgave her. The righteous might fall, but they can still stand in the judgment if they have the righteousness of Christ.

So even though you may not be Samson, Eleazar, or David, just remember that they didn't stand in their own strength. God helped them stand, and He can give you the strength too. Someone once asked Moody if he had enough faith to be tortured for Christ without denying Him. He answered, *"Not now I don't, but when that day comes I trust He'll give me the strength."* The Lord promises, *"As thy days so shall thy strength be"* (Deuteronomy 33.25).

STANDING ON THE ROCK

Jesus reinforces this truth in His parable about the wise man that builds his house on the rock. It's not only important to have the right foundation; we need the right materials like faith, hope and love—materials that He provides us. Will your house stand? By repenting and believing that by Christ's blood we are innocent, we can be counted worthy for His sake—and be left standing.

We Christians have some trials ahead. The last thing we need is our church becoming complacent during a time when our lamps should be trimmed. And we need to have something genuine; we need to know Him to stand. We need to be able to sing like Jehoshaphat's choir, singing God's praises and standing still in His salvation.

Let's look again in our Bibles. Revelation 14:1 says, *"And I looked, and, lo, a Lamb stood on the mount [Zion], and with him an hundred forty and four thousand, having his Father's name written in their foreheads."* But if we're going to be able to stand with Him then, we need to stand in faith now. I want to be among those. How about you? I want to stand before the Lord, clad in His armor and covered by His blood.

There may be some of you who realize that your foundation is made of the wrong stuff and today you'd like to begin building on Christ. So I'd like to end on this last promise, found in 1 Thessalonians 3:8: *"For now we live, if ye stand fast in the Lord."*

CONCLUSION

"*Commit your way to the Lord, Trust also in Him, And He shall bring it to pass.*" –Psalm 37:5

When a bride and groom stand before the minister, they make some very broad and permanent vows ... promises that are meant to last forever. What gives them the confidence that they can fulfill these vows? They have a strong love and a deep sense of commitment. In the same way, when we make our baptismal vows we should understand that this means "In sickness and health, in prosperity and adversity, in the sunshine and the rain." God's church family will have many of the same highs and lows of any earthly family, but if we love Jesus and commit to love His people, it becomes a precious experience that will survive any trial.

I think we sometimes underestimate how much God can do through one completely converted, *committed* Christian! Through the prayers and faith of one ordinary man, Elijah, the nation of Israel was turned back to God. The Bible promise is:

"The effective, fervent prayer of a righteous man avails much. Elijah was a man with a nature like ours, and he prayed earnestly that it would not rain; and it did not rain on the land for three years and six months. And he prayed again, and the heaven gave rain, and the earth produced its fruit."
–James 5:16-18

King David also reminds us, "***Commit*** *thy way unto the Lord; trust also in him; and he shall bring it to pass*" (Psalms 37:5, emphasis mine).

Paul adds, "*For I know whom I have believed, and am persuaded that he is able to keep that which I have* **committed** *unto him against that day*" (2 Timothy 1:12, emphasis mine).

And of course, the example of complete commitment is Jesus. "*Who, when he was reviled, reviled not again; when he suffered, he threatened not; but* **committed** *himself to him that judgeth righteously*" (1 Peter 2:21-23, emphasis mine).

Here is one of my favorite statements on commitment. It's from
E. G. White, one of our greatest Christian writers:

*"The greatest want of the world is the want of men—men who
will not be bought or sold; men who in their inmost souls are true
and honest; men who do not fear to call sin by its right name;
men whose conscience is as true to duty as the needle to the pole;
men who will stand for the right though the heavens fall."*

–Education, p. 57

Dear friend, I've learned that with God's help, a person can do
almost anything he or she wants, if the desire is really there. I have
also learned that where there is faith and hope, all things are
possible to him that believes. If you truly desire and believe, you can
survive and succeed in church as a vibrant, Spirit-filled Christian.

However, without Jesus we will surly sink in the stormy times
ahead.

Friend, this is the only way to survive the tempest ahead: Have
Jesus in your boat. Let Him take the ropes and rudder and He will
lead you through the storms of life and safely bring you to heaven's
harbor.

So, I implore you to make a firm commitment today . . . to ask
Him to be your Captain, Lord and Savior and to fill you with His
Spirit . . . and then faithfully follow Him wherever He leads.

You've read how God used Elijah to share His amazing grace—
and the amazing results that followed. Now just imagine what
millions of last-day Elijahs calling people to Jesus throughout the
entire world will do. I hope and pray that you will be one of these.

Why not join me now in making this pledge of commitment to
Jesus by choosing to put your hand to the plow, holding tight, and
never looking back?

*"But Ruth said: Entreat me not to leave you, Or to turn back
from following after you; For wherever you go, I will go; And
wherever you lodge, I will lodge; Your people shall be my people,
And your God, my God. Where you die, I will die, And there will
I be buried. The Lord do so to me, and more also, If anything but
death parts you and me."*

–Ruth 1:15-17

AMAZING FACTS

Visit us online at
www.amazingfacts.org
and check out our online catalog
filled with other great books, videos,
CDs, audiotapes, and more!

Don't miss our FREE online
Bible Prophecy course at
www.bibleuniverse.com
Enroll today and
expand your universe!